THE ROAD

Cormac McCarthy

AUTHORED by D. Dona Le
UPDATED AND REVISED by Adam Kissel

COVER DESIGN by Table XI Partners LLC
COVER PHOTO by Olivia Verma and © 2005 GradeSaver, LLC

BOOK DESIGN by Table XI Partners LLC

Published by GradeSaver LLC, www.gradesaver.com

First published in the United States of America by GradeSaver LLC. 2009

ISBN 978-1-60259-198-1

Printed in the United States of America

For other products and additional information please visit http://www.gradesaver.com

Table of Contents

Table of Contents

Biography of McCarthy, Cormac (1933-)

Cormac McCarthy's works revel in the shadows of human nature, but Cormac McCarthy had a remarkably conventional childhood. He was born Charles Joseph McCarthy in Providence, Rhode Island, on July 20, 1933. He later changed his name to Cormac, meaning "son of Charles," to honor his father. His family moved to Knoxville, Tennessee, in 1937. His father, a lawyer, took a job with the Tennessee Valley Authority legal staff and remained with the TVA for the next thirty years. Even though his childhood biography might seem to have no defining moment or climactic event that would shape his career, a number of key themes in Cormac's works--peregrination, the human affinity for bloodshed, and issues in father-son relationships--had their place in his formative experiences.

Cormac grew up in the Catholic church, attended Catholic high school, and enrolled at The University of Tennessee in 1951. He completed only one year, however, before deciding to enlist in the U.S. Air Force. He served four years in the military, two of them on duty in Alaska, before returning to the University of Tennessee in 1957. He found himself slowly gravitating towards fiction writing. After publishing two stories in *The Phoenix*, the campus literary magazine, he won an Ingram-Merrill Foundation grant for creative writing in both 1959 and 1960. Convinced of his potential for success, he left the university in 1960 to pursue his writing career.

McCarthy moved to Chicago and became an auto mechanic to support himself while he worked on his first novel. He married Lee Holleman, with whom he had one son, Cullen McCarthy. Soon afterward, he returned to Tennessee with his wife, but the marriage dissolved.

Such personal troubles seem not to have distracted him from his work. McCarthy published his debut novel in 1965, *The Orchard Keeper*, and was recognized with the William Faulkner Award. The novel, published by Random House, was edited by William Faulkner's editor, Albert Erskine.

McCarthy has not enjoyed sustained critical success and support. In 1965, he won an American Academy of Arts and Letters traveling fellowship to Europe and boarded an ocean liner to Ireland. On the trip he met Anne Dulsie , whom he married in England in 1966. That same year, he was awarded a Rockefeller Foundation grant, allowing him to tour Europe with his wife. After traveling through England, France, Switzerland, Italy, and Spain, the McCarthys settled in Ibiza, a Spanish island, so that Cormac could finish revising his second novel, *Outer Dark*.

In what seemed like a routine, McCarthy won another fellowship in 1969, the Guggenheim. He moved with his wife to Louisville, Tennessee, where he fully renovated a barn into a home while leisurely working on his third novel, *Child of God*. During the mid 1970s, he wrote the screenplay for a PBS film, *The Gardener's Son*.

In 1976, McCarthy separated from DeLisle and moved to El Paso, Texas. Perhaps unsettled by the changes in his life, McCarthy returned to the familiarity of his creative nemesis, *Suttree*, a manuscript with which he had been struggling for twenty years. His perseverance was rewarded in 1979. Critics hailed the book as his finest (some argue that he never surpassed it), and he was awarded the prestigious MacArthur Foundation Grant. Meanwhile, McCarthy and DeLisle divorced in 1981.

If critical accolades were a mainstay of McCarthy's career, popular success was not. But with the 1985 publication of *Blood Meridian*, his work began to gain mainstream attention. Declared one of the best novels of the twentieth century by critic Harold Bloom, *Blood Meridian* perhaps best captures the bleak cynicism at the core of McCarthy's body of work. In chronicling the escapades of a young runaway who joins a bloodthirsty gang in their Indian hunts, *Blood Meridian* reveals the darker shades of human character, the inevitability of suffering and violence.

McCarthy has no reason to apologize for these dark themes. In a rare interview with the *New York Times*, he seemingly rejects not only the possibility for harmonious living, but also the idea that human beings can seek to change their aggressive instincts: "There is no such thing as life without bloodshed. The notion that the species can be improved in some way, that everyone could live in harmony, is really a dangerous idea. Those who are afflicted with this notion are the first ones to give up their souls, their freedom. Your desire that it be that way will enslave you and make your life vacuous" (*New York Times Magazine*, 1992). Accepting that people have their faults, that is, points us away from unachievable utopian ideals and leaves us free to be ourselves as we really are.

One of McCarthy's better-known novels is the first novel of his so-called Border Trilogy, *All the Pretty Horses*. This novel also depends on its characters swirling in the maelstrom of unforeseen, inescapable evil. Despite its bleak themes, the book built upon the acclaim of *Blood Meridian*, meeting with both critical attention and commercial success in 1992. In addition to remaining a *New York Times* bestseller for six months, it won the National Book Award and National Book Critics Circle Award, further evidence that critics were practically unanimous in declaring it the best work of fiction that year.

McCarthy then published the two remaining books in The Border Trilogy: *The Crossing* (1994) and *Cities on the Plain* (1998), the latter of which unites the two lead characters from the first two books in the series. During the same year *The Crossing* was published, McCarthy also edited and published a play entitled *The Stonemason*, which he had written during the 1970s.

Though the exact year is unclear, McCarthy entered his third marriage around the time of publication of *Cities on the Plain* with Jennifer Winkley. Since then, the couple have had one son, John Francis McCarthy.

In recent years, McCarthy has once again garnered new critical acclaim and Hollywood attention with his two latest works, *No Country for Old Men* (2005) and *The Road* (2006). (*All the Pretty Horses* had been adapted into a film in 2000, but it had met with generally negative reviews.) *No Country for Old Men*, released in film by the Coen brothers in 2007, was widely acclaimed and received a multitude of awards, including Academy Awards for Best Picture, Best Director, and Best Adapted Screenplay.

The Road was awarded the James Tait Black Memorial Prize for Fiction in 2006 and, in 2007, the Pulitzer Prize for Fiction. Since then, the novel has been adapted to film and was released in 2009. *Blood Meridian* has also been adapted to the big screen and is currently classified as in production.

Rarely granting interviews, reliably silent about his work, McCarthy did concede to his first television interview with Oprah in June 2007, after she named *The Road* as her April 2007 Book Club selection. McCarthy currently lives north of Santa Fe with Jennifer and their son, and he satisfies his interest in science by spending time as a research fellow at the Santa Fe Institute.

About The Road

The Road (2006), Cormac McCarthy's most recent novel, describes the bleak journey of a father and son across a post-apocalyptic American landscape. He was visiting El Paso, Texas, with one of his sons, John Francis McCarthy, in 2003 when the initial idea for *The Road* was born: McCarthy envisioned how the city would look in the future. McCarthy dedicated this novel to John.

The novel has met with great critical success, including a Pulitzer Prize and the James Tait Black Memorial Prize. Many critics and scholars herald *The Road* as one of McCarthy's best works--if not his masterpiece. Extensive praise for *The Road* can be found on his publisher's (Random House's) webpage for the novel. Oprah Winfrey selected *The Road* for her Book Club in April 2007, which led to McCarthy's first televised interview on her program later that year.

McCarthy's literary repertoire includes revisions of various genres, including the crime thriller (*No Country for Old Men*) and the Western (the Border Trilogy). Some readers entertain an ongoing debate regarding whether *The Road* should be classified as fiction, science fiction, or even horror, given McCarthy's brutal prose and unflinchingly vivid vision of what could be considered a hell on earth. Nonetheless, most agree that *The Road* is a deeply moving, if also deeply disturbing, work of unparalleled literary genius that transcends any discussion of genre.

Character List

the man

The man (also referred to as the father, who is called Papa by his son) travels the road with his young son. He believes he has been appointed by God to protect the boy, and he does so at all costs, even killing another human being in order to save his son. Unlike his son, the man remains deeply suspicious and even paranoid of other individuals and their intentions--perhaps understandably so. He is loath to approach other travelers on the road to offer them assistance, while the boy often wishes that he would. The man grows sicker throughout the novel, and his illness is manifested in his persistent cough and bloody spit. At the end of *The Road*, the man dies next to a stream in a clearing in the woods.

the boy

The boy (also called the son or the child) is born into the post-apocalyptic world. He knows nothing about the world before the catastrophe. He travels the road with his father and believes that he and his father are the "good guys" who carry the fire. In various encounters with other travelers on the road, the boy continually displays his faith in humanity and his humbling trust in others. Despite their near brushes with brutal violence and death, the boy consistently pleads with his father to help others in need. After his father's death, the boy is rescued by a family of people who assert that they are also the good guys.

the burnt man

The father and the son encounter a man on the road whose footsteps have left tracks in the road tar. The man has been struck by lightning and is heavily burnt. The boy wishes to stop and help the man, but his father refuses, insisting that they are unable to help him in any way. At last sight, the burnt man has collapsed on the road. This experience greatly upsets the boy, who does not talk to his father for a period of time due to their disagreement and the sad result.

man from the truck

This man becomes embroiled in a violent encounter with the father and his child. After exchanging words in which the man attempts to cajole the protagonists into joining his group, the father rightly does not trust him. The man grabs the son, holding a knife to his throat. The father promptly shoots the man in the head, killing him.

the man's wife

The wife of the man who is the protagonist has already died, and her situation is only described in flashbacks. She chose to avoid rape and murder, which she believed were inevitable, by committing suicide. She used a piece of sharpened obsidian, since the family's pistol only had two bullets. She did not say goodbye to her son, and she killed herself despite the entreaties of her husband not to do so.

the little boy

The son sees a little boy during their journey and runs after him, calling out to assure him that he and his father mean no harm. The father, however, forbids his son from pursuing the boy. As he felt regarding the burnt man, the son is again devastated that his father would not allow them to pursue and assist the boy. Even after they leave that area, the son wonders what will become of the little boy and who will take care of him.

the naked people

Inside a padlocked room in a grand house, the father and the son stumble upon a horde of naked people. They are imprisoned there to be used as food by four men and two women who are cannibals. The naked people beg the protagonists for assistance, but the father and the son must run away in order to escape the cannibals.

the cannibals (four men and two women)

These people control the large house that the protagonists happen upon. They are cannibals who entrap people in the house and lock them in the padlocked room, where the people are later killed for food.

Ely

Ely is the only person on the road with whom the protagonists have extensive contact. Upon the boy's pleading, the father agrees to give Ely food and allows him to camp with them for one night. Later, Ely tells the protagonists that he has not given them his real name. He longs for a world without any humans, where death itself would be lonely.

three men with pipes

The protagonists run into three men who are armed with pipes. They are outmatched by the father's pistol and must let the man and his son pass by without harm.

three men and a pregnant woman

When the man and the boy encounter a small group of people, three men and a pregnant woman, the protagonists hide, but their arrival frightens these people into hastily leaving their camp. The people leave behind the remains of their dinner, a burnt infant. When the man initially saw them out in the darkness, however, there was no infant, suggesting that the pregnant woman has attempted to eat her own child along with her cannibalistic companions.

the thief

The thief tries to steal the protagonists' cart and other belongings from their beachfront camp. The man tracks him down and threatens him with the pistol. Though the boy wants to help the thief, the man forces the thief to strip naked and takes his clothes and shoes. Later, at the boy's insistence, the man and the boy return to where they left the thief on the road, in order to return his clothes.

a man shooting arrows

While passing through a town, the protagonists are attacked by a man shooting arrows at them from a house. The father sets the house on fire with a flare pistol. It is unclear whether or not he kills the man, though they hear the man's screams from outside. When the boy asks his father about it later, the father responds that he did not kill the arrow man, and he promises his son that this is the truth.

a woman

When the father enters the house from which the arrows were shot, he encounters a woman holding the arrow man.

the man with a shotgun

A man with a shotgun appears near the conclusion of *The Road*. He extends a welcoming and helping hand to the boy, now that his father has died. This individual brings the boy back to his family, which includes his wife and two children, a boy and a girl.

wife of the man with a shotgun

This woman helps take in the boy and welcomes him to their family. From her brief appearance, she is portrayed as religious. She encourages the boy to talk to God and teaches him that God's breath is passed from man to man. She thus serves as a kind of redemptive figure for the boy.

Major Themes

Death

Death and the specter of death pervade *The Road* from the onset through descriptions of the landscape, the protagonists' struggle to survive, and the constant threats of murder and starvation. The earth is already steeped in death and ashes. Most living creatures and plants have not survived the disaster that has destroyed civilization. For example, cows are extinct, and the boy has never before seen birds or fish. "On the hillsides old crops dead and flattened. The barren ridgeline trees raw and black in the rain" (18).

Death is also personified as a lover (48) and as an entity which will meet its own demise (146).

As the novel progresses, the reader becomes more acutely aware that the man is dying. "In the night he woke in the cold dark coughing and he coughed till his chest was raw.... He knelt there wheezing softly, his hands on his knees. I am going to die, he said. Tell me how I am to do that" (148). His encroaching death, evidenced by his worsening cough and the increasing amounts of blood he spits out, stalks the reader.

Even descriptions with rich colors and textures serve as reminders of death. When the man dreams of his wife, of his life before the universal destruction, he considers these dreams to be the call of death beckoning him from the bleak reality of his present life. These brief passages throughout *The Road* only highlight the world's inertial motion towards death, a force that also seems to drive the protagonists on their journey, especially for the father.

Paternal love

The theme of paternal love is ubiquitous given the relationship of the two protagonists. As the man's wife points out before her suicide, "the boy was all that stood between him and death" (25). In other words, the man's thirst for survival is fueled by the love for his son. While the man may expect his own death, he lives in order to seek life for the boy. Unlike his wife in her suicide, the man does not wish to "save" his son from civilization's destruction, rape, murder, and cannibalism by killing him preemptively. To the father, suicide is only an option for the son if he is to be imminently harmed. Perhaps for this purpose he leaves the pistol with the boy whenever he explores a new and potentially unsafe location alone.

The man's love for his son does drive him to ensure his son's survival. The man frequently demonstrates the strength of this love, most obviously in his unflinching decision to shoot and kill the man who threatens the boy's life. Throughout the entire journey, the man does not kill out of malice or for food. He only hurts others (the man who attacks the boy and the thief who takes their cart) when they have threatened the boy's survival. His wariness toward others, which is well justified, seems primarily for the protection of his son.

In less dramatic and violent situations, the man gives his son as many "treats" as he can in such a world--an old can of Coca Cola, a powdered drink mix. As the man lays dying, he tells his son to eat his share of food, instead of keeping it for himself in hopes of regaining his health. These small gifts and sacrifices are strong examples of his paternal love.

Good versus Evil

The theme of good versus evil is perhaps most appropriate for a post-apocalyptic novel. This theme may be more explicit in *The Road* than in any other McCarthy novel. More than once, the boy seeks confirmation from his father that they are the "good guys" and that the "bad guys" are those who seek to hurt them--thieves, murderers, and cannibals. According to the man, the good guys are those who "keep trying. They dont give up" (sic, 116). A symbol of the goodness in human perseverance and hope is the "fire" that the father assures his son they carry. As a "good guy," the man and the boy carry the fire internally, meaning that they strive to live under all circumstances.

In such a world, however, the conflict between the good guys and the bad guys is not at all clear. To the father, they are the "good guys," even though the father commits a murder for the sake of his son. The man does not consider acting violently in defense of his son's survival evil. Yet, what makes this choice more praiseworthy than the choices of the people who kill and even cannibalize others in order to survive?

Indeed, the boy does not understand the need to hurt others in any circumstances, even when they may pose a danger to his own survival or have already hurt him. For example, the boy pleads for his father to spare the thief and, even more, to help him. Because he is complicit in the father's punishment of the thief (stripping him of his clothes and shoes), the boy no longer feels like one of the "good guys." He feels that the stories his father tells of their heroic survival are not truthful. Perhaps worst of all, the boy cannot agree with his father that the right thing to do is to refuse to help others who are in dire need, especially when they have not shown any evidence of being dangerous. The reader (if not also the boy) perceives that in such a difficult world, the distinction between good and evil is rather nuanced; people's actions taken at face value are far from enough to determine whether someone is a "good guy" or a "bad guy."

Trust

Issues of trust figure prominently throughout *The Road*, particularly with regard to the man's relationship with his son. On the surface, this theme is expressed through the conflicts between the protagonists and other people they encounter on the road. For example, the man who draws a knife on the boy initially attempt[s to] coax the father into joining his comrades at their truck. The father rightly does no[t] trust this man--appropriately, since the man attempts to harm the boy only seconds later. In fact, the father does not trust any other individual they see or meet. Only his son extends his humbling trust in others, offering to help Ely and the thief without first determining whether their intentions are malicious.

More subtly, McCarthy also explores issues of trust between a father and his son, here between the man and the boy. The boy looks to his father not only for information but also for guidance and reassurance. Though he often seeks reassurance, the boy also realizes that his father may not always be truthful about their chances of survival. The boy admits that he thinks his father might lie to him about dying, to which the father responds, "Okay. I might. But we're not dying" (McCarthy 86). The man also questions the boy's trust regarding the issue of "good guys." Disillusioned by his father's treatment of others on the road, the son does not believe his father's pronouncements that he and his son are the good guys.

Toward the end of the novel, the son no longer wants to hear his father's stories because he deems them untrue. In a brief but telling exchange, the boy tells his father: "I always believe you.... Yes I do. I have to" (Mccarthy 156). In this respect the son's trust in his father is forged out of necessity. The man is the boy's only companion and authority figure, and he knows about the nature of human life before the unnamed catastrophe. The father's longer years and longer experience make it impossible to fully discount the father, so the son has reason to trust him in addition to the fact that he must count on his father for protection.

Faith and Doubt

Religious faith--and religious doubt--figure prominently in this novel. At times, the father's quest south to ensure his son's survival is carried out with religious fervor: "the child was his warrant. [The man] said: If he is not the word of God God never spoke" (4). When Ely expresses surprise at meeting a child, the man counters, "What if I said that he's a god?" (145). Indeed, the man treats his son as an individual above all others, with a devoutness that arguably surpasses the usual sentiments of paternal love, affection, and protection.

In other instances, however, the man expresses doubt about, or at least questions, the existence of a higher power. "Then he just knelt in the ashes. He raised his face to the palling day. Are you there? he whispered. Will I see you at the last?" (10). Ely goes further and outright denies the possibility of God's existence in such a destructive place as earth ("There is no God and we are his prophets," 143), whether or not divinity is incarnated in the boy. "Where men cant live gods fare no better. You'll see" (sic, 145).

The boy's own religious faith remains ambiguous. When Ely asks whether his son believes in God, the man replies, "I don't know what [the boy] believes in" (146).

e boy's faith in God is practically irrelevant compared with his trust in evidenced when the woman whose family rescues him at the novel's attempts to teach him about religion. "He tried to talk to God but the was to talk to his father" (241). The boy carries "the fire" of which his ke, the fire of hope and human resilience.

Survival and Resilience

Strong attention to the practical aspects of human survival, what resilient people do in order to survive, are perhaps to be expected in a post-apocalypic novel like *The Road*. These commonly include man's inventive efforts to use the remaining natural resources or trashed items to survive. McCarthy tends to focus on the unusual behavior required in such circumstances, for example of the marauders or cannibals--behavior that might seem crazy in any context other than one in which people feel that they must abandon the most basic principles of morality just to stay alive.

Survival is not the only option, however. The man's wife, in an effort to escape rape and murder, chooses to take her own life before her life and integrity are taken from her against her choice. The man also attempts to steel himself for the possibility that he may have to shield his son from unspeakable evil by killing the boy himself. "Can you do it? When the time comes? When the time comes there will be no time ... Could you crush that beloved skull with a rock?" (96).

Yet, most people in *The Road* have apparently chosen malicious means of survival, becoming murderers. Some of these individuals are less violent, such as the thief from whom the father strips his clothes and shoes. Others, however, are cannibals who appear to have reconciled themselves even to eating human infants.

Still others have banded together to form small but no less destructive militias. These individuals wage a merciless war for survival against everyone who is not part of their group. "Behind them came wagons drawn by slaves in harness and piled with goods of war and after that the women, perhaps a dozen in number, some of them pregnant, and lastly a supplementary consort of catamites ..." (78). Here we see the beginnings of a new society arising from a state of nature, one where the security of the group is the key binding motivation.

In the face of the atrocities they witness, the boy and the man retain a purity of hope and strength of vision that fuel them forward in their journey across the desolate land. In particular, the boy's capacity to believe in others' goodness is staggering. His spirit and hope remain resilient against the gruesome scenes he witnesses or experiences. Though the man is less trusting and more aware of the potential dangers of their journey, he too retains his humanity and does not stoop to the deplorable acts committed by the thieves and cannibals. He has a moral resilience that trumps his mere survival instinct.

Narration: Naming and the Authority of Memory

The Road incorporates significant themes regarding memory and narration. These themes are often difficult to grasp through McCarthy's obscure language or references and almost impenetrable prose, but it is important to remember that thought and memory are seldom so clear as the words of a treatise. One might argue that in *The Road*, memory and narration create realities, whether or not these memories or narrations are accurate. Storytelling and naming, accordingly, are forms of authenticity and power, lending reality to those objects or concepts which are described or named. "Make a list. Recite a litany. Remember" (27).

In one way, this theme is exemplified by the man's dreams and memories of his life before the destruction of civilization. Though the man attempts to reject his dreams as death's lure away from the sobering reality of his impending end, these dreams in some way validate the existence of his previous life, the existences of "things no longer known in the world.... He thought each memory recalled must do some violence to its origins.... What you alter in the remembering has yet a reality, known or not" (111). This passage also demonstrates the significance of memory for a person; the mind remembers and thus validates phenomena which may no longer exist. Failing to remember and to name these phenomena render them forever lost.

Interestingly, however, the man and the boy remain unnamed throughout the entire novel. The only person who is named, Ely, reveals that this is not his true name and explains that "I couldn't trust you with [my name]. To do something with it. I dont want anybody talking about me. To say where I was or what I said when I was there" (sic, 144). He suggests here that naming expresses the namer's power to create and determine a reality, one which the named may not agree with. Thus, by remaining unnamed, the protagonists and even Ely retain a measure of autonomy over themselves--their identities, actions, and stories. There is thus a limit to what the reader can draw from their words and actions; the unnamed man is a kind of "everyman." McCarthy lets them, in the imperfect way an author can, speak for themselves, and the reader, in the imperfect way a reader does, must remember and retell their stories with incomplete information.

Glossary of Terms

alabaster

a white and translucent material commonly used for vases and ornaments; the white color of the material

bandolier

a broad belt worn over the shoulder and across the front of the body, commonly holding gun cartridges

bolus

a round mass or lump, especially of chewed food; a drug dose administered intravenously

cauterize

to burn a cut or similar wound for healing purposes; to deaden

coagulate

to congeal or clot; to thicken from a fluid into a denser mass

creosote

a flammable, oily liquid derived from coal and the tar procured from wood

derelict

abandoned or deserted, especially by the owner or occupant

effigy

an image or representation of a person; a crude representation of a disliked person

entabled

relating to entablature, the superstructure of a building in Greek or Roman architecture, supported by columns

Formica

a brand of plastic used most commonly for surface finish

gullied

having undergone erosion, usually by running water, to form a small valley or ravine

hemlock

a poisonous plant of the parsley family, characterized by small white flowers and finely cut leaves; a poisonous or lethal drug made with this plant

intestate

of a person who dies without having executed a valid will; of an object which is not disposed of according to a valid will

Krugerrand

a one-ounce coin from the Republic of South Africa

litany

a form of prayer marked by invocations or supplications, alternating with responses by the congregation; a tedious recitation or account

lode

an ore deposit, or an abundant supply or source

mastic

a Mediterranean tree or its aromatic resin, which can be used as an adhesive or a varnish

midden

a pile of refuse or trash, indicating human settlement

Pajaro de Esperanza

(Spanish) bird of hope

palisade

a fence of stakes or sharp posts used as a defensive barrier

phalanx

in ancient Greece, a group of heavily armed infantry formed in ranks and files; a closely massed arrangement of bodies or things

pipsissewa

a small evergreen plant with shiny green leaves, able to be used as medication

port cochere

(from French) a porch wide enough to allow a vehicle and its passengers to arrive and enter under the building's cover

predicated

founded or based upon

promontory
a high point of land or rock which overlooks or projects over lowland or a body of water

provenance
place of origin; the history of ownership of a valued object, such as a work of art or an antique

runic
like or featuring runes, the seemingly strange characters from one of the alphabets used by Germanic peoples from the third to the thirteenth centuries; possessing a secret or mysterious meaning

sepulchre
a place of burial, a tomb

soffit
the underside of a part of a building, such as a beam, arch, or cornice

souwester
a hat or slicker made of oilskin, most commonly used by seamen in rough weather

swale
a shallow, wetter depression in the land

tarpaulin
a durable material or cloth used to protect an exposed object or area

Thespian
relating to Thespis, a sixth-century BC Grecian who is credited with being the first known actor, particularly in tragedies; any actor

translucent
describing an object that permits light to pass through it, but diffusing the light enough so that objects cannot be seen clearly through it; somewhat comprehensible, but not as clear as what is transparent

Short Summary

The Road describes the journey south taken by a young boy and his father after an unnamed catastrophe has struck the world. The man and the boy, who also remain unnamed throughout the entire novel, travel through the rough terrain of the southeastern United States. The conditions they face are unforgiving: rotted corpses, landscapes devastated by fire, abandoned towns and houses. These two travelers are among the few living creatures remaining on earth who have not been driven to murder, rape, and cannibalism.

The father and his son struggle to survive in the harsh weather with little food, supplies, or shelter. Along the way, they must escape from those who might seek to steal from them or, even worse, to kill them for food. Despite their hardships, the man and the child remain determined to survive, reaffirming to themselves that they are the "good guys" who do not seek to harm others. The boy in particular retains his unquenchable humanity against all odds, consistently seeking to help the tattered remnants of living humans they encounter.

Unfortunately, the father's health worsens as they travel, and by the time they reach the ocean, he is near death. He continually coughs up blood, and the two are forced to move at ever slowing rates each day. Finally, he dies in the woods lying next to his son in the middle of the night. The boy remains by his side for several days after his death, but eventually the boy meets a kind family who invite him to join them. The boy must say goodbye to his father and embark on a new journey with this family.

Quotes and Analysis

"The world shrinking down about a raw core of parsible entities. The things slowly following those things into oblivion. Colors. The names of Things to eat. Finally the names of things one believed to be true. More fragile than he would have thought. How much was gone already? The sacred idiom shorn of its referents and so of its reality."

75

The first sentence here indicates that the post-apocalyptic world has been reduced to basic elements, "a raw core of parsible entities," where complexity is a luxury. More sophisticated aspects of human civilization have been obliterated, and the names of such things are slowly being forgotten by the remaining humans, following the things themselves into oblivion. Such things include colors, types of birds, and certain foods. More importantly, fundamental truths and customs regarding human life have been lost. These perhaps include the capacity to hope, or to feel empathy, love, and altruism. These concepts, once "believed to be true," are in fact "[m]ore fragile than he would have thought," too easily lost in the new reality. Significant principles and the words that signify them ("sacred idiom") are forgotten and lost; the objects and concepts themselves cease to be. One can infer from this vision that the process of naming and storytelling lends reality to the object or concept being named and described, while in the absence of naming, memory, or narration, the object or concept no longer exists in a way that has human meaning.

"... there is no other dream nor other waking world and there is no other tale to tell.

On this road there are no godspoke men. They are gone and I am left and they have taken with them the world. Query: How does the never to be differ from what never was?"

27

The first sentence of this quotation alludes to the theme of narrative power. Only one tale can be told, and this tale legitimizes or brings to reality only one waking world ("no other dream nor other waking world"). The second section of the quotation offers a hint as to what kind of catastrophe might have struck the world. On the road that the boy and the man travel together, no "godspoke men" exist. The term "godspoke men" may allude to prophets, which arguably align with Ely's statement (see the seventh quotation below) later in the book. The prophets are gone, having "taken with them the world," which suggests that some kind of religious war has destroyed human civilization, or that whatever happened has completely destroyed the moral world, the moral principles that commonly are seen as religious

Yes.

The final statement in this short quotation first places an emphasis on the importance of the present. The man also adheres to the importance of the present; he does not wish to be attracted to his dreams of false happiness, nor does he enjoy being affected by memories of his dead wife and past life. Those who seek the "never to be" entertain deluded hopes, the falseness of utopia, while those who yearn for "what never was" similarly maintain meaningless illusions; both harm one's capacity to focus upon the present, and in this aspect, they do not differ. If the resurrection or Messiah or nirvana has never really come in this world, if these are the only end times, there is not really any role for "godspoke men" anymore; this is the one, awful world.

"The one thing I can tell you is that you wont survive for yourself. I know because I would never have come this far. A person who had no one would be well advised to cobble together some passable ghost. Breathe it into being and coax it along with words of love. Offer it each phantom crumb and shield it from harm with your body."

49

These lines are spoken by the man's wife as they discuss her intended suicide and what she projects to be his future with their son. The wife rightly points out that man's drive to survive will be fueled by his love for the boy. In other words, in order to survive in the post-apocalyptic chaos and destruction, love for another human being is required. Someone who does not love another individual would be "well advised to cobble together some passable ghost" of a loved one. The way in which the man's wife describes how this ghost should be treated is exactly how the man treats his son. He shields the boy from harm and offers him "phantom crumb[s]" of whatever hope and sustenance he can find, whether it is an outdated Coca Cola or half a tin of canned fruit, and he constantly encourages the boy to survive "with words of love." His moral and literal survival depend on being concerned for the boy.

"You wanted to know what the bad guys looked like. Now you know. It may happen again. My job is to take care of you. I was appointed to do that by God. I will kill anyone who touches you. Do you understand?

Yes.

He sat there cowled in the blanket. After a while he looked up. Are we still the good guys? he said.

Yes. We're still the good guys."

65

This brief conversation demonstrates the depth of the man's love for his son, while simultaneously revealing the son's growing concerns about their actions as the "good guys." The lines occur after the man has shot and killed the attacker who threatened the boy with a knife at his throat. The passage also underscores the underlying difference in morality between the man and the boy. To the man, his killing is justified because it was committed in the act of saving his son, a responsibility he says (and may well believe) was assigned to him by God. The boy, however, is concerned about the nature of the act, regardless of the circumstances. He wonders whether, having murdered someone, they can still be considered the good guys. This seed of doubt is evident in the boy's mind, since he must ask the question at all, but the father unequivocally still considers them good, or at least wants to reassure his son that he feels that way, protecting his son at all costs.

"He walked out in the gray light and stood and he saw for a brief moment the absolute truth of the world. The cold relentless circling of the intestate earth. Darkness implacable. The blind dogs of the sun in their running. The crushing black vacuum of the universe. And somewhere two hunted animals trembling like groundfoxes in their cover. Borrowed time and borrowed world and borrowed eyes with which to sorrow it."

110

This vividly desolate passage reveals the utter indifference of the universe to the plight of man, a cosmic condition that he takes to be the "absolute truth of the world." The earth continues to revolve, "cold" and "relentless," indifferent to the sufferings of its inhabitants. Furthermore, the earth is "intestate," a word used to describe a person who has died without leaving behind a legitimate will. In other words, in its own death from whatever calamity has struck, the earth has left no future, no means of survival or compensation for its survivors. Even the sun is blindly indifferent in the midst of the "crushing black vacuum of the universe," which extends far beyond the human world of just the earth and the sun. Yet the survivors really exist for the moment, somehow. The hunted animals probably represent the man and the boy, living in spite of the universe's disinterest, witnessing this wasteland with their fleeting lives.

"Maybe he understood for the first time that to the boy he was himself an alien. A being from a planet that no longer existed. The tales of which were suspect. He could not construct for the child's pleasure the world he'd lost without constructing the loss as well and he thought perhaps the child had known this better than he."

129-130

This passage more explicitly describes the power of storytelling to create realities. The father tells his son "tales" about life before the catastrophe which has rendered the earth a wasteland to its survivors. However, to the son, these tales are hard to believe because they are so unlike the current reality. The father, having experienced the pre-apocalyptic world, is thus alien to the son, who knows only life after the disaster. The earth enjoyed by the man during his own childhood is a "planet that no longer existed" to the boy. When the man considers attempting to make this old world real to his son by telling stories about what used to be, he realizes that the story is too difficult and sad to tell; the whole story is a story that ends in loss. His son, perhaps, knows that the story of the old world ends with the present world, that his father's nostalgia cannot reproduce that older world unless the story leads them right back to where they are.

"There is no God and we are his prophets."

143

In an atheist reversal of the usual religious theme of prophets, Ely suggests that he and others are here to preach the central message of the reality of this world: that it is the only world, and a sad one at that. Prophets are necessary in order to correct the usual ways of the world. If the atheists are prophets, it is because they are correcting an error such as human hope. In this view, humans shape civilization of their own accord and do not possess any divine comprehension of life or of the universe. To Ely, it seems that the universe is so indifferent to humans that humans need to learn this basic lesson in order to honestly confront reality.

"Do you think that your fathers are watching? That they weigh you in their ledgerbook? Against what? There is no book and your fathers are dead in the ground."

65

These lines also call into question the existence of a higher power and of an afterlife. The speaker indicates that the actions of humans on earth are not witnessed or weighed by a higher power--or even by those who have already lived and died. If there is a moral center, it is not defined by the principles once held by the dead, but by the individual, perhaps. A person is the final judge of his own actions.

Going further, the narrator rejects any notion of a ledgerbook, the traditional metaphor for a moral record of one's actions for use by divine judges. This utter rejection of religious belief thrusts the novel further into a world in which man's capacity for evil and violence is not wholly unguided and unchecked by outside forces and in which individuals, in their natural state, do not even keep their own score in terms of morals. Ledgerbooks and ideas about being watched and judged by outsiders are the complex human constructs that artificially guide morality in an impotent effort to explain or to regulate behavior. A man must be a law unto himself if there is to be any law at all.

In addition, by calling upon "fathers" instead of "mothers" or "ancestors" in general, McCarthy further emphasizes the paternal theme in *The Road*.

"You're not the one who has to worry about everything.

The boy said something but he couldnt understand him. What? he said.

He looked up, his wet and grimy face. Yes I am, he said. I am the one."

218

The man occasionally thinks of his son (or explicitly refers to him) as a godly product. Even his mission to protect the boy and to ensure his survival is carried out with religious fervor and described in religious terms. Yet, this response is the boy's only acknowledgment in the novel that he may in fact be a kind of "chosen one." Perhaps the boy does realize that the world's humanity does depend on his own survival, since he metaphorically carries the fire (in Greek mythology, Prometheus steals fire and brings it to mankind, for which he is punished). He is the representative of the remnant, the new generation that might lead to a new, peaceful civilization. If he is to have this role, he does have the weight of the world, of everything, on his shoulders. The man's intimation of his son as a godlike, redemptive figure seems to be more than zealous paternal love, and the son has the hope and resilience to perhaps make this world worthwhile again.

"You have to carry the fire.

I don't know how to.

Yes you do.

Is it real? The fire?

Yes it is.

Where is it? I dont know where it is.

Yes you do. It's inside you. It was always there. I can see it."

234

As he lays dying, the man has this conversation with his son, who wishes to be able to die with him, but he tells the boy to persist, to survive and carry the fire. This fire, the kind found within the self, is a symbol of everlasting hope and human resilience. Instead of succumbing to the circumstances and resorting to evil acts to survive, the boy carries the fire and does not compromise his higher human morality. The boy demonstrates that he carries the fire throughout the book, since no matter what horror they narrowly escape, the boy always seeks to help other individuals and never believes they should be hurt or punished, even if hurting others might ensure his own survival.

This allusion to "carrying the fire" may be more than a reference to the dangers of Promethean fire. It also might refer to McCarthy's previous novel, *No Country for Old Men*, in which one character dreams of his father carrying fire. "I knew that he was goin on ahead and that he was fixin to make a fire somewhere out there in all that dark and all that cold and I knew that whenever I got there he would be there" (*No Country*, 309). Human fire brings hope to confront the bleak future of the post-apocalyptic world.

To the extent that the novel resonates with the real world as readers find it, the message is the same: people like the boy always carry the fire. The sad truth, however, is that the world is all too much like the one in *The Road*, with far too many people seeming to choose self-preservation at the cost of genuine human concern for others. Our more complex world is not so simple as the tradeoff involved in killing others in order to survive, but McCarthy points out to us our human nature--the fire of human compassion is all too easily extinguished when we encounter adversity.

Summary and Analysis of Section 1

These sections are divided using the Picador edition (2006). Section 1 extends from the beginning of the novel to the end of page 24.

The Road opens with the man, one of the novel's two central, unnamed protagonists, awakening at night to check on his sleeping son. Even in sleep, the man and the boy wear facemasks. The man has been dreaming about wandering in a flowstone cave, led by his son, "Like pilgrims in a fable swallowed up and lost among the inward parts of some granitic beast" (3). In the dream, the man and his son arrive at a "black and ancient lake" across from a blind creature (3). The creature is translucent, and its innards are vaguely visible. The creature turns away from the man and the boy.

At dawn, the man leaves his makeshift bed with the boy to investigate the land, "Barren, silent, godless" (4). He does not know what month it is, though he guesses the season is autumn. The reader understands that the man and his son have been on the move for at least a year. The man uses binoculars to search for any signs of life, but he finds none.

When the boy awakens, his father is already by his side with food ready. The father believes their location is unsafe during the daytime because they are visible from the road. With their shopping cart and backpacks, which carry their most necessary belongings, the boy and his father travel the dead land, heading south.

They come across an abandoned gas station, and the father decides to check if it still bears any useful objects or tools. He finds nothing of use. The description of the gas station, as well as of the overall landscape, reeks of bleak desolation and abandonment. The father picks up the phone and dials what used to be his own father's phone number. They leave the station, but the father quickly returns and removes all of the oil bottles from the trash in order to collect as much motor oil as possible. They will use the oil for their lamp. The boy says that his father will now be able to read him a story.

As they continue to travel, the landscape remains charred, dead, abandoned. "[T]he shape of a city stood in the grayness like a charcoal drawing sketched across the waste. Nothing to see" (7). It starts to rain, so the father leaves the shopping cart in a gully, protected by a tarp, and he sits underneath a rock overhang with his son to stay dry. After the rain stops, they retrieve their cart and make camp. They survey the city below from the top of a hill to check for signs of fire or light, but they see none. They prepare for bed. The son is too tired to have his father read to him, but he asks to keep the lamp on until he falls asleep.

Before falling asleep, the boy asks his father whether they will die, to which his father replies, "Sometime. Not now" (9). He adds that if his son were to die, he would also wish to die so that they could be together. After his son falls asleep, the father remains awake listening to the nothingness of the world.

Again, the father wakes before dawn and before his son. He looks to the sky, perhaps futilely questioning God. "Have you a neck by which to throttle you? Have you a heart? Damn you eternally have you a soul?" (10).

They pass through the city, the father holding their pistol close by. They see a corpse. The father remembers an idyllic day from his childhood with his uncle.

For weeks, the two continue south as the weather grows colder and the nights grow longer. The terrain is particularly brutal and barren; they cannot make fire. One day, it begins to snow. They discover a roadside garage in which they are able to make a fire and repair one of the shopping cart wheels. They continue in the morning, and as they pass a barn, they discover three bodies hanging inside. The boy wishes to scavenge for items they might need, but his father does not allow him.

They continue their journey. The father dreams of his dead wife, "out of a green and leafy canopy" (15), in stark contrast to the black and gray ashes which surround them in the daytime. He does not trust his dreams, believing that they are "the call of languor and of death" (15). But even when awake, he continues to think of his wife.

The father constructs sweeps to add to the cart, to clear the road before it. He uses the cart with his son sitting inside like a bobsled, and finally his son smiles. They come across a dam and a lake, and the father tells his son there are no fish in the lake. As their journey continues, day after day, the father's dreams grow more vivid. From an old billboard they see for Rock City, the reader can assume that they are near what used to be the state of Georgia.

They stop at a farmhouse, where the father takes bedsheets and blankets. At an abandoned supermarket, the father finds a Coca Cola can, which he gives his son as a treat. In yet another city, they encounter countless more corpses.

One day, they arrive at the house where the father grew up. The boy is frightened and does not want to enter the house, but his father does. The rooms in the house are empty, but they are still as the father remembers them. He can imagine the way Christmas used to be, and how he spent time with his sisters. He shows the boy his bedroom. The experience deeply frightens the son, and they leave.

Three nights later, they experience an earthquake. The description here reveals that during this time, many refugees traveled through the barren land as do the father and his son.

The two of them settle in an abandoned house, where the boy sleeps and the father reads old newspapers from a lost time.

Analysis

From the very first page of *The Road*, McCarthy's distinct writing style fits the world he describes. Most obviously, his punctuation is extremely sparse. McCarthy does not use apostrophes to indicate contractions (for example, he uses "dont" instead of "don't"), and he does not use quotation marks to set apart dialogue from exposition. The conventions of writing hardly matter in this post-apocalyptic world. Moreover, the dialogue is usually set apart from exposition as a new indented line, but occasionally, some dialogue runs into the exposition as well. For example: "His face in the small light streaked with black from the rain like some old world thespian. Can I ask you something? he said" (9).

Further, in the above quotation, one can also see that McCarthy's prose often includes sentence fragments. In other cases, a lack of commas and other punctuation creates run-on sentences: "He dreamt of walking in a flowering wood where birds flew before them he and the child and the sky was aching blue but he was learning how to wake himself from just such siren worlds" (15). McCarthy's stark prose style here reflects the barrenness of the landscape. The relentless consistency of this writing style helps create and sustain the mood of the book and its world, which is discussed in further detail below.

The reader spends the first section only with the man (called "Papa") and his son, the boy. Thus far, they are the only live characters in the book; the various antagonists they will encounter have not yet appeared. But the father hints at the others' presence, making sure that their pistol is within reach and that they are not followed or seen by others. "He kept constant watch behind him in the mirror" (21).

The initial and most obvious conflict the protagonists face is the struggle to survive in a destroyed and destructive landscape. It is the conflict of man versus nature, with the old civilization providing tools. The father and son must scavenge for food and other vital supplies. In this section, the environment itself is the antagonist. They must battle against the harsh fall and winter, the rain and snow. The dry and ashen land, seemingly bereft of any other life, maybe even plants, makes their journey even more difficult.

The opening section of *The Road* thus quickly captures the dark mood of the novel. The novel's second sentence already indicates the bleakness of the world these protagonists inhabit: "Nights dark beyond darkness and the days more gray each one than what had gone before" (3). Throughout the novel, additional details of the landscape reinforce this bleak image of the protagonists' environment. "The blackness he woke to on those nights was sightless and impenetrable.... No sound but the wind in the bare and blackened trees" (13). The general mood that quickly permeates the book is one of death and desolation, and the plot bears this out.

To punctuate this mood, the father and his son are also preoccupied with death. The reader cannot avoid the worry. The son asks his father whether they will die; the father believes his dreams are the lure of death. Interestingly, this perception of his dreams is paradoxical, as only in these dreams or reminiscences so far does

McCarthy allow for any "life" in his descriptions. The dreams are made vivid and lifelike, in stark contrast to the deathly environment. "He dreamt of a flowering wood where birds flew before them..." (15), or "he'd watched a falcon fall down the long blue wall of the mountain [with its] blowsy plumage in the still autumn air." The birds and falcons, the colors, are now gone. Moreover, the father believes they are symbols of death: "How else would death call you?" (18).

The father also appears to treat his child as a redemptive figure: "[The father] knew only that the child was his warrant. He said: If he is not the word of God God never spoke" (4). This statement alludes to the man's religious hope; his love for his son seems to come from a divine commandment within him. Indeed, much of the plot revolves around the father's paternal, hopeful efforts to keep his son alive despite everything.

Summary and Analysis of Section 2

Section 2 covers pages 25 to 59.

The father and son continue traveling south as winter descends. They expect to travel across mountains, and the father hopes they have enough food. They travel in snow but make campfires at night to keep warm. In the distance, they can see forest fires raging in the mountains. One night, as they make camp, the father watches his son stoke the fire, "God's own firedrake" (26).

In the morning, the fire in the mountains is still visible, but the weather grows colder. They continue south. The father dreams that his wife is sick and he cares for her. Though the dream seems sacrificial, the father remembers that "she died alone somewhere in the dark" (27).

The narrative switches briefly into a flashback to describe what occurred apocalyptically on earth, though not explaining why. "People sitting on the sidewalk in the dawn half immolate and smoking in their clothes... Within a year there were fires on the ridges and deranged chanting. The screams of the murdered" (28).

The father, who is familiar with this part of the land, expects to reach a summit soon. Finally, he recognizes the location he seeks. They stop to rest, and the father makes his son hot cocoa, while he drinks only hot water himself. The boy reminds his father that he promised not to limit himself like that, so the father splits the hot cocoa among them both. The son tells him, "If you break little promises you'll break big ones" (29).

They plod onward. When the road is obstructed by fallen trees, they must unpack their cart, carry their belongings to the other side, then repack it. At night, the boy has a nightmare about a wind-up penguin that haunts the house they used to live in, moving without being wound up.

It takes four days for them to travel out of the snow. They discover a river with a waterfall. They bathe in the waterfall, despite the cold. In the woods, they find morels (a kind of mushroom), then settle down for the night, satisfied with their makeshift camp.

In the morning, the father checks for other people and once again finds none. After staying at this camp for an undisclosed amount of time, at least several days, the father decides they must leave because the waterfall will attract others. They consult an old, dismembered map and plan their route. The man tells the boy that the area used to be divided into states. The boy, having been born and become aware of the world after whatever the catastrophe was, does not know about the states and wonders what happened to them. The father cannot answer him.

They make their way to a bridge that crosses the river, but a jack-knifed tractor trailer blocks the way. The father must maneuver their cart of belongings underneath the truck. They sleep there that night, then investigate the trailer the next morning. The father climbs into the trailer, only to discover "bodies. Sprawled in every attitude" (40).

The man and the boy camp that night in the woods. The boy is frightened by brief lightning. The next morning, the father notices a fire in the horizon. They continue to walk and see a set of footprints in the burned and cooling tar. Eventually, the man and the boy catch up with the footprint-maker and follow him. The man looks burnt because he has been struck by lightning. The boy wishes to help the man, but his father refuses, thus upsetting the boy. Eventually, the burnt man collapses "and at that distance you couldnt even tell what it was" (43).

One day, the father empties his wallet of money, old credit cards, his driver's license, and a photograph of his deceased wife. He throws away the wallet, then lays his wife's picture on the road and leaves. Later, he reminds his son that they could not have helped the burnt man in any way. Their exchange indicates that the son has been upset with his father for some time and has not spoken with him--but this episode is over. That night, the father dreams that he is called by a group of figures on the far shore of a river.

In a few very short flashback sequences, the fate of the man's wife and the boy's mother is revealed. The first flashback describes a time when the woman was pregnant with the boy. All of the clocks stopped at 1:17, the power went out, and through the window, the father saw a "dull rose glow" (45). Most likely to collect water in the event they would run out of water as well as power, the father stopped the bathtub and ran both taps on high. Another memory of the man involves hearing birds overhead. "He never heard them again" (45).

As they travel, the man tries to teach his son card games he has long forgotten. The father thinks about his wife's picture, abandoned on the road, and wishes he could keep her with them in some way. He awakens one day, coughing up blood, and wakes up his son. The boy wants his mother, and his father replies, "You mean you wish that you were dead.... You musnt say that" (47).

The next flashback involves a conversation between the man and his wife after the boy has been born. At this point, the family has struggled to survive, like "the walking dead in a horror film" (47), for some time. They are survivors, and the man entreats his wife not to commit suicide. She wishes to die by her own hand, however, in order to escape what she believes is her inevitable rape and her family's inevitable murder. She wishes that their pistol had three bullets, not only two, so that she could spare her entire family from their gruesome fate. Throughout the conversation, the man continues to beg her to reconsider her decision, or at least to wait until the morning to say goodbye to their son. She refuses and leaves. The man knows that she commits suicide by sharpening a flake of obsidian, "[s]harper than steel. The edge an atom thick" (49). In the morning after her death, the man and the boy pack up their camp, and the boy only says, "She's gone isn't she?" (50).

In yet another flashback, the boy's birth is described: "in their bed by the light of a drycell lamp. Gloves meant for dishwashing" (50).

One day, the father awakens alert, pistol in hand. He sees people approaching, "wearing canister masks. One in a biohazard suit. Stained and filthy. Slouching along with clubs in their hands, lengths of pipe" (51). Farther down the road comes the noise of a truck. The father quickly hides their belongings and runs away with the boy. The men in the truck pass them, but the truck sputters to a stop. The men in the truck dismount in order to push it past the slope. The father sees a man from the truck standing only twenty feet away.

The father pulls the pistol on the man and tells him to approach them, warning him not to call to the others or else be shot. The man was in the process of sharpening his knife on his belt. The father questions the man about where he and his crew are going, whether their weapons have ammunition, and so on. The man does not believe the father will shoot him because of the boy's presence. He correctly guesses that the father has only one or two bullets (he has two). The father does not like the way the man looks at his son. The man attempts to cajole the father and son into joining them with promises of food.

The confrontation comes to a nasty climax when the man dives for the boy, "holding him against his chest with the knife at his throat" (56). The father shoots the man in the head, then grabs his son, puts him on his shoulders, and runs away. They continue on their journey, freezing cold, the man coughing. "They neither spoke nor called to each other, the more sinister for that" (57).

They continue to stumble through the woods. The father worries that they only have one bullet left. The boy's hair is streaked with the man's blood, and he refuses to talk to his father. After more walking, they come across the road they were on, which yields the tire tracks of the truck. It presumably has continued on its way without the man who was shot.

Analysis

McCarthy offers further clues regarding the novel's setting in the middle of this section, making an allusion to "the states" (36). Readers will infer that this wasteland was once the United States of America, a governmental system that presumably dissolved in the apocalyptic disaster. The man cannot explain to the boy why the states were dissolved, but the roads remain.

The man's act of leaving his wife's photograph on the road is richly symbolic. His wife chose to commit suicide rather than travel the road with her family in search of safety and survival, but the man deposits her picture on the road instead of dumping it somewhere else. Thus the man acknowledges that she was on the road with them in his mind and in some way is still on the road, but he finally is leaving her behind. She may be on some other path toward her own salvation; they indeed have parted ways. She chose to die, and he chose to live. Yet, when he leaves the photograph behind along with his wallet and his contents, he is admitting a kind of defeat for the old world. He had been keeping these elements of the old world together with him, but now that he has failed to help the burned man, he realizes that he can no longer keep up the idea that there is an old world to hope for. He lost some part of his humanity by not even trying to help, and so now he leaves behind the symbols of his old life, even the photograph of his wife.

McCarthy intersperses flashback sequences in this section to describe fragments of the man's life before the catastrophe and to explain what happened to the man's wife. These flashbacks disrupt the story's normal chronology, which generally follows the little boy and the man in the present, and returns the narration to the past. By employing flashbacks, McCarthy does more than offer background information to help us understand the tragedy and the man's present thought and emotions. Since the flashbacks are not clearly separated from the rest of the narration, they intentionally obscure the story's linearity and reflect the man's shifting between memory and reality. Just as the flashbacks make the novel's present more difficult for the reader to grasp in some ways, the man drifts in and out of dreams and memories. This disjointed narration technique helps sustain the novel's mood of confusion and isolation.

This section also features various literary devices in McCarthy's descriptions of nature. For example, he writes about the "fireblackened boulders like the shapes of bears..." (25) and "the banished sun, "which "circles the earth like a grieving mother with a lamp" (28). These similes render the descriptions more vivid and poignant. Likewise, trout are described as "[r]eflecting back the sun deep in the darkness like a flash of knives in a cave" (35). These negative comparisons further perpetuate the negative tone of the story. In addition, an example of hyperbole occurs in the line, " it was so quiet they could all but hear their hearts" (29), emphasizing not only the desolation of the scene but also the desolating effect on their hearts, their humanity.

The boy's dream about a wind-up penguin gone out of control may be an allegory for the catastrophe that has struck the earth. In the dream, the boy is frightened by a wind-up penguin that is able to stalk their own home of its own accord, without being wound up by the father. Originally, the penguin only runs after the father winds it up. This toy perhaps symbolizes man's creations, at first under man's control but soon taking on their own agency and getting out of control (its "winder wasnt turning," 31). In other words, man's creations became a destructive, uncontrollable force. This dream thus could refer to whatever event caused the earth's tragedy—the disaster was in some sense of man's own making, perhaps a reference to the religious fanaticism that comes when people make up their own gods and then are willing to kill one another on behalf of them, or some similar way that human technology and artificial desires got out of control and led to war.

The primary conflict in this section occurs between the man from the truck and the protagonists. Initially, the danger presented by the man from the truck is ambiguous. Though the father is deeply suspicious of the man's intentions, the man acts conciliatory, offering to let the father and the son join his band. However, the sincerity of his offer is questionable, and the father's suspicions are vindicated when that man pulls a knife on the boy. The exchange reaches its violent climax when the father feels forced to protect his son by shooting the man in the head to kill him. For the father, the moral choice is unpalatable but easy: it is acceptable to kill his son's attacker in order to save his son. His son, perhaps too naive, is not so sure, which creates a new level of moral conflict between the father and the son.

In this section we also see the father's illness coming up, to the point that he coughs up blood and wakes his son. This is an element of foreshadowing of the father's ultimate death from the illness. For now, however, the father will persevere. Staying put will probably do no good, after all.

Given that the son was not born before the tragedy began, it must have occurred years ago, yet there are still corpses and destruction everywhere, with roads and buildings still standing, and with supplies to some degree still available. It seems that even to this day, people are killing one another and leaving corpses, which explains why the father is so clearly justified in being wary of anyone they meet. Also, it seems as though the world might have been suspended for some time, with people emerging only after a time in order to start picking up the pieces. This suggests some sort of nuclear holocaust, with the survivors somehow hiding and then finally emerging when they thought the radiation levels were low enough. Such a speculative idea is supported by the recollection of "[p]eople sitting on the sidewalk in the dawn half immolate and smoking in their clothes," although other vehicles of war could have the same effect. But we do not know what really happened; we simply find the characters now in this new, awful world.

Summary and Analysis of Section 3

Section 3 covers pages 59 to 82.

The father is unsure whether the people from the truck have left for good or are lying in ambush. The man and the boy come across the truck crew"s old campsite, which is still warm, so the father instructs his son to stay put while he investigates. The father finds the cart of his and his son"s belongings. It was plundered, and only a few of the boy"s belongings remain. The father notices that the truck crew are cannibals; they left behind boiled bones.

The father and son return to the bridge to make camp, and the father goes to retrieve wood for a fire. The boy is frightened. Later, the man sits down to make dinner. He then bathes the boy to rid his hair of the remnants of the dead man"s blood and brains.

The next day, they once again set out. The father expresses regret over what happened with the man from the truck: "I should have been more careful" (65). He tells his son that those were the "bad guys" and assures him that they are and will always be the "good guys." During their journey, the father carves a flute for his son, who begins to play it.

They survey the valley below them for signs of life, and the boy spies smoke. The father decides they must investigate, despite the danger, because they need food. After passing through an abandoned store, the man scavenges suit coats. Unfortunately, they find nothing else of use or value at the store or in the abandoned houses at the edge of the town.

On the way back to their camp, they hear a dog. The man promises his son they will not kill it, but they never hear the dog again. They sleep that night inside a parked car, and when they wake up, they manage to find some utensils, clothes, and plastic to use as a tarp. The father feels as though they are being watched, but they see no one.

After they eat, the boy suddenly notices someone looking back at him from a house across the street. The son sees another little boy about his age and runs after him. "Come back, he called. I wont hurt you. He was standing there crying when his father came sprinting across the road..." (71). As with the burnt man, the son wishes to help this boy, but the father refuses because the threat of danger is too high. Again, the boy becomes extremely upset and claims he does not care whether he dies. The father apologizes and tells him he must not say such a thing.

As they continue on, the boy asks his father whether the other boy has anyone to look after him. The son remains deeply moved by the incident and still wants to help the boy. "We could go back, the boy said softly. It"s not so far. It"s not too late"

(73). The man recalls another incident from back when his wife was still alive. At that time, their family came across another dog. The father considered killing it, but his wife walked away, and the boy had begged him to spare the dog"s life.

Their slow and painful journey continues. The father guesses that the month is November. They find an orchard with "a frieze of human heads, all faced alike, dried and caved with their taut grins and shrunken eyes" (76).

One morning, the father awakens to see a large group of people marching up behind them. The man and the boy hide close to the ground, where they are not visible from the road. The people continue to march onward, all of them carrying deadly weapons such as chains and spears and lances, as though bearing "wagons drawn by slaves in harness and piled with goods of war" (78). The two escape notice, however, and resume their journey. The climate grows unbearably colder, and the snow worsens, falling quickly.

They make camp and struggle in the falling snow to retrieve wood for the fire. The father goes to fetch wood, and his son follows him to help. At night, the man is in despair over his son"s "sunken cheeks streaked with black" (81). He awakens from his sleep because of the sound of falling trees, and he decides that they must quickly depart. They find another place to sleep.

Analysis

An important contrast in this section is between the cannibalism of the men who boil bones, on the one hand, and on the other hand the fact that the father washes away the blood and brains of the man he shot. In both cases, the unwanted body parts are gotten rid of. But the bad guys kill and eat people, while the good guys kill only when necessary and then try to remove the awful reminder of what they have done.

One passage in this section employs anthropomorphism of nature and natural elements to heighten the descriptions. McCarthy writes, "it burned with a frail blue flame and he ... watched the fire climb upward..." (61). Fire, an important theme in the novel, is thus anthropomorphized, as "frail" is an adjective usually applied to people. While the verb "climb" is a common metaphor for rising fire, it evokes the higher moral aspirations of the human heart. The climbing flame, however, is frail, like the fragile morality of the father, representing humanity in its most positive incarnations. The fire symbolizes the capacity for hope and the ability to love, both qualities which the man and especially the boy possess—as the "good guys"—qualities that are deeply challenged in their experience.

McCarthy also, perhaps, alludes to the pied piper (a well-known German legend) in this section. The initial legend of the pied piper describes him as a deathly figure whose pipe music lures children away to their disappearances and presumed deaths. McCarthy may invoke this image when the man constructs a makeshift flute for the boy. Behind the man, the boy "seemed some sad and solitary changeling child announcing the arrival of a traveling spectacle ... who does not know that behind him the players have all been carried off by wolves" (66). If this analysis is correct, McCarthy reverses the image of the pied piper in that the boy is a benign piper and a child himself who does not realize the damage his playing has done. He does not seek to bring his invisible followers to their deaths, but ironically they are "carried off by wolves" without his knowledge. This also alludes to human technology having unintended consequences.

In one paragraph from this section, McCarthy switches seamlessly between different narrative points of view. Though most of the narration is told from the third-person perspective, focusing primarily on the man"s perspective, McCarthy uses the first-person perspective in this paragraph (74). In fact, he changes the narrative style within one sentence, which is jarring and very unusual in literature: "The dog that he remembers followed us for two days" (74). The use of "he" implies third person narrative, while "us" switches to first person. We seem to be inside the head of the father in a different way. Indeed, the dog is significant in explaining the father"s moral vision. A dog is unlikely to want to kill and eat a person, even in desperation, it seems, or at least a dog is easily defended against. Thus it is ok to encounter a dog without attacking it, in contrast to all people, even children, who cannot be trusted to be safe.

Other literary devices used in this section are the rhetorical question, anthropomorphism, and onomatopoeia. The rhetorical question, intended to make a statement rather than to ask a genuine question, appears in, "More fragile than he would have thought. How much was gone already?" Although it is a genuine question for the reader, the question is meant to automatically signal that the answer is that very much is already gone, an unspeakable amount. Next, as seen in the last section, McCarthy anthropomorphizes nature when he writes that the "snow whispered down in the stillness and the sparks rose and dimmed and died in the eternal blackness" (81). There is something haunting about a humanized nature in such a desolate context. Finally, examples of onomatopoeia also occur, as they commonly do, in descriptions of nature, such as when the trees in the woods are falling in the snow. "The whump of the falling trees and the low boom of the loads of snow" (82) employs onomatopoeia with "whump" and "boom."

Summary and Analysis of Section 4

Section 4 covers pages 83 to 107.

The snowfall is deep, and the man and the boy struggle to retrieve their cart. When they finally find it, they must leave it behind because of the snow. The man first makes better footwear for the boy and for himself, using the suit coats and plastic. Traveling through the snow is exceedingly slow and difficult. The boy continually asks about their impending deaths, struggling. The father is too weak to carry him. There are not enough daylight hours to travel far, and the snow impedes their speed.

One morning, they discover wagon wheel tracks in the snow. The father is afraid that the tracks are from "bad guys," and they attempt to cover their tracks in the snow as well as possible. The man selects a high campground so that they can survey their surroundings. As expected, he sees two men traversing the road, but these men continue on their way without disturbing the protagonists.

After five days of no food and hardly any sleep, the man and the boy stumble upon a large house outside a small town. The father wants to investigate the house, noting that there are no tracks leading up to it from that direction. The house used to be grandiose and impressive; now, they find heaps of clothing and old sleeping bags. The boy is terrified inside the house but accompanies his father. The ashes in the fireplace are cold.

The father finds a steel padlock blocking the entrance to a door. The son wishes to leave, but the father insists upon hacking open the padlock with a spade. He is desperate to search for food for their survival. Inside the room, the father finds countless people, "naked people, male and female, all trying to hide, shielding their faces with their hands" (93). One man's legs have been amputated up to his hips, and the room reeks. The people beg the man for help. The man drops his lighter in his haste to leave the room, hurrying his son along with him. They slam the door behind them to leave.

Just then, across the field, the boy and his father see four men and two women approaching. They run away as quickly as possible, but the six people are quite close by. The father hands his son the pistol and tells him that, if necessary, he must commit suicide. "You know how to do it. You put it in your mouth and point it up. Do it quick and hard" (95). They remain in hiding as night falls, when the father hears "hideous shrieks coming from the house" (97).

The father realizes that the house is a trap. A box near the road allows people to watch for those like himself approaching the house, so that they can warn the others of the newcomers' arrival. The newcomers are then trapped in the padlocked room and kept for food for the cannibals.

In the middle of the night, the father and the son run away through the woods, hoping that they do not accidentally circle back to the house. Dazed, not knowing their location, they must press forward in the morning. The man regrets the danger in which he put himself and his son, thinking about the house and the padlocked room. "It was desperate that had led him to such carelessness and he knew that he could not do that again. No matter what" (99).

Leaving the boy sleeping, the father goes to investigate a barn, where he takes seeds from the bales of hay for food. He enters a house near the barn and finds a flavored powder with which to make drinks, and he takes it with him. He also takes away a screwdriver and a new blade. Near the barn, "he stood there thinking about cows and he realized they were extinct" (101). He finds an apple and eats it entirely, then realizes that he has come upon an apple orchard (there are fruitful plants after all). The father collects as many apples as he can. Back in the house, he also discovers a good water source. "He lay there a long time, lifting up the water to his mouth a palmful at a time" (103). The father empties jars from the kitchen to fill them with water.

He returns to the boy, still sleeping, with the apples and the jars of water. When the boy wakes up, they eat together, and the man makes the powdered drink for his son. Later that day, they collect more apples from the farmhouse and fill more jars of water. They endure an extremely difficult night in the cold. They cannot make a fire because the man had dropped his lighter earlier. The boy seeks confirmation from the father that the people from the first house were going to eat them, thus validating why he and his father could not have helped them.

Analysis

If this is Georgia in November, the snow represents a drastic climate change somehow related to the tragedy. As far south as they are, the weather is a major antagonist for them. The towns are the most dangerous places, even if they provide buildings that can offer shelter from the weather, for that is where cannibals and others tend to remain, in wait for newcomers to kill and eat. The orchard at least provides apples, so the prospect of benefiting from nature has not entirely disappeared. The scene with the apples and water provides a ray of hope, strongly contrasting with the ultimate despair of the naked humans who are the food of cannibals.

The boy's first reaction to that house foreshadows the terrible discovery they make and the gruesome fate they narrowly avoid. When the man and the boy first stumble upon the house, the boy has a bad feeling and does not want to enter the house. Even as they continue to explore the house, the boy's misgivings do not fade but increase. However, the father is relatively confident enough to continue searching the house for supplies. Here again the son perceives a moral reality that the father does not fully appreciate. Even in the face of the father's confidence, the reader still has the uneasy sense that the house may be dangerous due to the foreshadowing with the boy, and this disease is proved right when the truth is uncovered.

The people who run the cannibals' house are some of the most frightening antagonists the man and the boy face. They are a direct threat to the protagonists' survival. The four men and two women survive by trapping people in the house and keeping them there, slowly starving, to use as food later. The danger is quite real; they nearly catch the boy and the man, who fortunately manage to elude capture. This dramatic conflict is a major struggle between life and death, providing great suspense in addition to the horror of the situation itself.

The narration in this section is punctuated by rhetorical questions that emphasize the hopelessness of the protagonists' plight. "In what direction did lost men veer?" (99) underscores the realization that the man and the boy may be forever lost, that they have no direction. When considering the possibility that cows are in fact not extinct and that there may be one cow somewhere being cared for, the man wonders, "Saved for what?" (102). Again, this rhetorical question only underscores the sobering fact that there is no reason to save life, whether human, animal, or natural, in the post-apocalyptic world, except for its own sake, or else for personal love, like the father's love for his son.

Throughout *The Road*, the boy's reactions to the people whom they meet during the journey demonstrate how he and his father act as foils to one another. For example, in this section specifically, the man is not depicted contemplating their inability to assist the naked people who are awaiting their inevitable deaths. He in fact is unperturbed by this situation, amazingly hardened by past experience. His emotion is relief once he and his son have escaped. Yet, the boy is bothered by the fact that they are unable to help the naked people, just as he was upset when the father did not allow him to help the burnt man or the little boy. Unsettled, the boy seeks justification for their actions by confirming that they simply could not help the naked people without themselves being killed and eaten. It is very difficult for the boy to understand how it is possible to be a good guy when there are so many bad guys limiting their choices. We do not know why, but hopefully things are better wherever they are going.

Summary and Analysis of Section 5

Section 5 covers pages 108 to 135.

The boy seeks affirmation from the father that they would never resort to cannibalism, even if they were starving to death. His father reaffirms that they are the good guys and that they are carrying the fire. The father starts to lose hope each day as they slowly starve. "The country was looted, ransacked, ravaged. Rifled of every crumb.... He was beginning to think that death was finally upon them" (109). In the charred remains of a house, he retrieves a candle.

Near a small town, the man and the boy see an outdated sign that warns of death. The child tells the man he wishes the little boy from earlier in their travels were with them. At night, the father continues to have "[r]ich dreams now which he was loathe to wake from. Things no longer known in the world" (111). During the day, the father continues to be extremely cautious, holding the boy and their pistol close. He nearly lifts the pistol at their reflection in a mirror.

In a toolshed, the father finds packets of seeds, which he keeps. He also finds some gasoline. Nearby, he realizes that something is hidden underneath the grass. The man digs up the dirt and finds a door, and the boy becomes upset because he does not want his father to open the door. The two of them improvise a lamp and then return to the door in the ground.

Beneath the door, the man finds a bunker full of untouched food, along with other useful items like utensils. They enjoy a can of pears and peaches for dinner. The boy goes to sleep inside the bunker, while the man finds more useful items: clothes, soap, tools, toothpaste, and so on. Though he finds cartridges and rifle shells, he does not find a gun. Finally, the man also sleeps.

Upon awakening, the boy finally enjoys a proper meal of coffee, ham, and biscuits. The boy wants to thank whoever left behind all of this food, but he thinks he does not know how. "Yes you do. You know how to say thank you" (123). Finally, the boy offers a kind of prayer: "Dear people, thank you for all this food and stuff ... We're sorry that you didn't get to eat it and we hope that you're safe in heaven with God" (123).

The father heats up water to make a bath for his son. They both can finally clean themselves of the accumulated dirt and grime, then put on the new clothes they have discovered. The boy asks how long they can stay in the bunker, and his father answers that they must leave in a couple of days because it is dangerous. The man attempts to hide their location by putting a mattress over the latch door above them. While the boy sleeps, he whittles fake bullets out of wood to give their pistol the appearance of being fully loaded.

In the nearby town, they find a working shopping cart. Back at the bunker, the man cuts his son's hair and his own, then shaves. They enjoy another lavish dinner before going to bed. They stay at the bunker yet another day to eat and sleep, especially since the weather is rainy. The man and the boy collect what they will take from the bunker to load the cart. The next day, they leave.

The boy asks his father whether there are crows or cows, and his father says no. The father also reminds him that they survived their previously grim circumstances. He asks his son what happened to the flute, and the boy tells him that he threw it away.

As they continue, they see the remnants of a burnt city on the horizon. They stop on a hill, and the boy asks his father about their long-term goals, a phrase he heard from the man long ago. Neither of them knows what their long-term goals are.

Analysis

This section is primarily about new hope. Although the father is losing hope each day as they get hungrier, realizing that the houses have been thoroughly picked over, he maintains the fire inside. The one thing he retrieves, the candle, is symbolically important because it evokes hope. One the father begins to regain hope, he even asks about the flute, which the boy had thrown away, but with new hope comes a chance for a new flute. They can wash and eat and make a fresh start with a new cart.

McCarthy also displays the man's sense of bitter irony in this section. Instead of whittling a new flute, he whittles fake bullets. Similarly, when he almost smiles at the old sign warning of death, he realizes that the sign is blatantly pointless, given their circumstances. Death has already pervaded the world after the catastrophe, with humans resorting to indiscriminate murder in efforts to survive. Thus, what good is a mere sign when the reality is unmistakable in every direction?

In the towns through which the man and the boy pass, McCarthy describes many anachronisms, obsolete objects from the past that have no place in the post-apocalyptic world. For example, "through the paint could be seen a pale palimpsest of advertisements for goods which no longer existed" (108). Even billboards are obsolete, and the objects they advertise are anachronistic in this setting. Even the bunker seems anachronistic and out of place, an oddity in comparison to the wasteland all around, and it no longer serves its function of protection if at any moment, other people might come and attack the father and his son.

Very infrequently, McCarthy uses the second person in *The Road*. One example of this usage lies in this passage: "So be sparing. What you alter in the remembering has yet a reality, known or not" (111). The second sentence is not clearly delineated as one of the man's private thoughts, nor is it part of the dialogue. As part of the narration, this would indicate an address to the reader, warning us that reality actually extends beyond what we perceive or remember. We do not create and define things by remembering them and giving them names; this is an artificial alteration of reality. There is more than meets the eye, more than what can be described. Yet, much of a thing's reality for us is indeed bounded by what we perceive and say about it.

The man's use of an anachronistic figure of speech sparks a substantial dialogue between himself and the boy regarding crows. The figure of speech is "as the crow flies" (132). This describes a path of travel that is a straight line between two points. However, the boy is unfamiliar with this figure of speech and asks the man to explain it to him. There are no crows.

In this exchange, the crow serves as a metaphor for the boy's own hopes about what may be possible. He asks the father if a crow could fly to Mars or at least high enough to see the sun (132-134). These questions demonstrate the boy's willingness to hope for and to believe in the extremes of flight, what to us and to the father may seem impossible, especially for a crow. To some degree the crow symbolizes the boy himself, wishing to test the potential in his unknown future.

Summary and Analysis of Section 6

Section 6 extends from page 136 to page 158.

Ahead of them, the protagonists see a man slowly shuffling down the road. They follow him to determine whether he is a decoy for an ambush. Eventually, they overtake the old man. He is unkempt, filthy. "He looked like a pile of rags fallen off a cart" (137). The boy convinces his father to give the old man something to eat. The father allows the boy to give a tin of fruit to the old man. He tells his son they cannot keep the old man, but the child convinces his father to let them camp the night with the old man and give him a proper dinner.

The old man claims his name is Ely, though he later says this is not his true name. He claims to be ninety years old in order to protect himself from the bad guys--a tactic Ely admits does not always work. Ely has an extensive conversation with the man about the state of the world. "Nobody wants to be here and nobody wants to leave.... There is no God and we are his prophets" (143).

Ely does not consider people like themselves to be survivors, and he admits that he was surprised when he saw the little boy. The man replies, "What if I said that he's a god?" (145). Ely rejects this idea and insists that it will be better when all humans are dead. "When we're all gone at last then there'll be nobody here but death and his days will be numbered too. He'll be out in the road with nothing to do and nobody to do it to" (145-146). The next morning, the man and the boy--after some argument--give Ely some food and part ways with him.

The man's cough worsens as they continue to travel. He discovers that their tank with oil has leaked, since the boy forgot to turn both valves shut. The boy realizes this mistake, though the father pretends it is his own fault. For weeks, they travel as the landscape remains unrelentingly brutal. Onc day, the boy discovers an abandoned train, which they explore. At one stop, the man examines his maps and determines that they are approximately two to three weeks away from reaching the sea.

One night, the boy has a bad dream and wakes up his father. He has dreamt that he was crying and the man would not wake up. The man misunderstands and thinks his son is speaking of the present. The man and the child have a conversation about whether his son believes what he says.

Later, they encounter three men, armed with pipes, who ask them what they have in their cart. The father brandishes his pistol, attempting to look like an experienced killer, and continues on his way with the boy.

The father becomes ill with a bad fever, which frightens the boy greatly. They remain in one place for several days as the father waits out his sickness. He dreams of his previous life before the world's destruction. Finally, the man is able to rise and survey their surroundings from the top of the hill. He sees no signs of smoke.

Analysis

The man finally succumbs to the boy's goodhearted desire to help others. Perhaps because Ely looks too old and weak to be a threat, the father lets down his guard and even lets Ely camp with them for the night. The father seems to be feeling relatively rich with resources, quite the opposite of the way he felt when he was losing hope. He has the leisure and plenty to share. While the boy wants to help everyone, the father, hardened by reality, needs a greater measure of security before opening himself to helping others. Even then, his son must work hard to persuade him to trust Ely enough to help him.

Various clues point to the conclusion that the character of Ely, the only named figure in *The Road* (though he claims this is not his true name), is an allusion to Elijah the prophet. In biblical references, Elijah signifies the coming of the Messiah, the savior who will bring people out of their suffering. In the novel, this figure could be the boy, although Ely denies that the boy could be a god. Maybe Ely chose the name because of its similarity to "Elijah." Also, Elijah is first introduced in the Bible in 1 Kings 17:1. In *The Road*, when some part or the major part of the catastrophe occurs, the man notices that all of the clocks have stopped at 1:17. Perhaps this is another allusion to the Bible and the figure of Elijah, letting us entertain the interpretation of the mysterious Ely on the road as a prophet, much like other traditional prophet-like old men.

In Ely's conversation with the man, however, he personifies death. He says, "When we're all gone at last then there'll be nobody here but death and his days will be numbered too. He'll be out in the road there with nothing to do and nobody to do it to. He'll say: Where did everybody go? And that's how it will be" (146). If he is a prophet, he is a prophet only of the final act of destruction, not of some good on the other side of it. He describes death as a person, a figure who will presumably meet his own demise when his work on earth is complete. If he is a prophet of death, he is hardly needed, unless it is to extinguish the last hope of the so-called survivors.

In another passage from this section, McCarthy evokes religious imagery when describing the harsh weather the boy and the man face. He describes how the "secular winds drove them in howling clouds of ash to find shelter where they could," with "the noon sky black as the cellars of hell" (149). While "secular" refers to the state of being separated from religion, and thus this is a reference to their brutal indifference to their effects on people, the noon sky is compared to hell as though the relevant religious imagery is all on the negative side.

The abandoned train could be a symbol for the futility of man's efforts and technology in the face of nature's (and the universe's) indifference. "If [the man and the boy] saw different worlds what they knew was the same. That the train would sit there slowly decomposing for all eternity and that no train would ever run again"

(152). Despite the differing experiences of and the gaps in knowledge between the father and his son, both understand that the train is a representation of man's wasted efforts. The existence of man is fleeting and anachronistic compared with the eternal sweep of the universe's history; humankind will be outlasted by the timelessness of nature and its insensible violence.

The boy also describes a nightmare in which "I was dreaming. But you didnt wake up" (154). This dream foreshadows the circumstances in which the man will pass on at the end of the novel. The scene of the man's death is described later as follows: "He slept close to his father that night and held him but when he woke in the morning his father was cold and stuff. He sat there a long time weeping..." (236). The similarity between the dream and the actual circumstances of his father's death is clear. However, when the boy describes the dream, the father does not realize he is talking about a dream which foreshadows his own death, but he believes that the boy is talking about what just happened in the present.

Summary and Analysis of Section 7

Section 7 extends from page 159 to page 184.

The man remembers a winter long ago, when he was slightly older than his son's present age. He watched a group of men set fire to a mass of serpents in the ground.

One night, his son has a nightmare but refuses to describe it to his father. The man says, "When your dreams are of some world that never was or of some world that never will be and you are happy again then you will have given up" (160).

They continue to travel towards the sea, but the father is extremely weak. They come across a gruesome stretch of road upon which corpses lay "half mired in the blacktop, clutching themselves, mouths howling" (161). These people were killed on the road in a great fire. The father tries to prevent his son from looking, but the boy is surprisingly serene.

At a stop, the father and the boy think they are being followed. They decide to leave less trash behind so that anyone behind them will not know they have a food supply. They make camp, and while the boy sleeps, the father sees a group of people, three men and a pregnant woman, who pass them by. The next morning, the protagonists continue onwards.

They see smoke coming out of the woods, and the boy fears it is a trap. They smell cooking, and the man and the boy circle around it. Nothing remains in the woods, and the man surmises that the people were frightened of the man since they have a pistol. The people left quickly, their food still cooking, so the man and the boy examine the abandoned campsite. A shocking sight awaits them, which the boy notices first: "a charred human infant headless and gutted and blackening on the spit" (167).

They continue walking. During one stop, the boy says, "If we had that little baby it could go with us" (168). In the face of the horror they have recently seen, the boy apologizes for having shown serenity about the corpses burned into the road earlier.

They find a water source, and the boy runs ahead to drink from the water. The father notes that he has not seen his son run in a very long time. They filter the water and drink, but they have not eaten for two days.

They see a house in the distance. The man insists they walk to the house to search for food. On the way, the man finds a few arrowheads and gives them to the boy to keep. Inside the house, they find very old cans of food. They make a fire in the fireplace, make dinner, and spend the night inside the house. The boy begs his father not to go to the second story of the house, but the man goes nonetheless. They find clothes in the bedroom. The two of them stay in the house for four days, and the man makes new clothes for his son. They also find a wheelbarrow, which they use upon leaving to transport their new set of blankets and canned foods.

They continue. At a grocery store with gas pumps, they manage to acquire a cupful of gasoline. They start to run out of food once again, but the land they travel slowly changes. They finally reach the sea, but the ocean is not blue, which disappoints the boy. As they sit together on the beach, the boy wonders what lies beyond the ocean. The boy goes swimming despite the frigid weather. After swimming, the boy cries but does not tell the man why. They make camp near the ocean.

Analysis

The man's memory of the men who burn alive a great mass of serpents beneath a rocky hillside represents one of man's reactions to evil. "The men poured gasoline on them and burned them alive, having no remedy for evil but only for the image of it as they conceived it to be" (159). Just as with the snakes, human beings have met evil with destruction, themselves bringing forth whatever evil catastrophe has destroyed the earth. The men in the memory also have an "image of [evil] as they conceived it to be." The serpents represent "evil" or all of the negative circumstances people face. Snakes can't be transformed into something good; they can only be destroyed. The conclusion of this memory further emphasizes the men's callousness: "they disbanded in silence in the winter dusk each with his own thoughts to go home to their suppers" (159). Once the evil is destroyed, the people in the dream go back to their old ways, but in the present, the old ways are gone now that civilization itself has been destroyed.

Other reactions to evil are possible, too. This section of *The Road* demonstrates good examples of the boy's gradual character development. Earlier in *The Road*, the man usually instructs his son to turn his eyes away from the gruesome corpses they often see along the journey, and the boy wants to help people they meet. Here, they see the corpses of travelers who have been burned alive on the road's tar. Yet this time the boy is "[s]o strangely untroubled" (161). This calmer reaction suggests that the boy is maturing, not that he is callous but, like his father, knows which evils must be left alone. Later, the boy suggests to the father that they are being followed. This response to evil, wariness or flight, also demonstrates the boy's growing awareness of his surroundings and maturity. He is growing less dependent on his father for survival and comfort.

This does not mean that in leaving evil things alone, the boy loses hope. It is true that the dead infant being cooked on the spit obviously cannot be helped, but the boy somehow wishes that it could be alive, traveling with them. Earlier, the man and the boy encountered other cannibals, but this unspeakable monstrosity indicates the irreparable destruction of innocence and humanity. The next generation, for the cannibals, does not matter. The dead infant is a symbol of the utter death of man's innocence, and the boy has matured to the point that he knows his good motivations, his hopes, are going to be very difficult to fulfill. At least the hope of the ocean lies ahead.

McCarthy repeats the motif regarding the significance of naming and memory in this section. As the man surveys the road, he notes: "Rich lands at one time. No sign of life anywhere. It was no country that he knew. The names of the towns or the rivers" (170). Since the man no longer knows the names of the towns or rivers they are passing through, there is nothing to remember, and there is no new sign of life to produce a memory that matters.

As they cross a field, the man finds both an arrowhead and an old coin with Spanish lettering on it. The arrowhead is not a souvenir or interesting artifact so much as it is a symbol of human violence. In passing along the arrowhead to the boy, the father gives a private reminder of evil that complements the evil they see almost everywhere on their journey. In contrast, he drops the coin, which has no cultural value and is a reminder of what is lost. Human violence is one of the few things that did survive the catastrophe.

Of course, other essential elements of humanity have survived as well, and in part McCarthy has used this story to examine what does remain of humanity when almost everything of culture has been destroyed except for the objects themselves, which must be scavenged. Humans continue to scavenge hope; they continue to try to stay alive, many of them travel (and more or less in the same direction), and the man and boy have been on a mission to the south and the sea, even though they are not sure what they are going to do when they arrive.

At the end of the section, they reach a house with supplies that they make a haven for a short time. They seem more hopeful than before, not so paranoid about others finding them. They do, finally, reach the sea. Perhaps as expected, it is not so exciting, but the boy gives it a shot and goes swimming in the cold waters. When he cries, it is probably for several reasons. The ocean has probably not met his hopes. The swimming was ok, but now that they have arrived, is it really any better than where they were during their journey? It's not even blue. The sea is actually a huge barrier to further progress across the whole east, so it is a major limitation on the boy and his father, contrasting with its traditional boundlessness.

Summary and Analysis of Section 8

Section 8 spans pages 185 to 210.

While the boy sleeps, the man stands on the beach and reminisces about his life when his wife was still alive. When he returns to their camp, the boy is awake and frightened. In the morning, they explore the beach. They come across an abandoned ship. While the boy keeps lookout on the beach with the pistol, the man swims out to the boat to explore it.

The ship is named *Pajaro de Esperanza*, or *Bird of Hope*, and hails from Tenerife, a Spanish island. The boat has not been ransacked, and while the sea apparently has destroyed most of its contents, it turns out that much remains. The man is able to retrieve some clothes for himself and the boy. He also recovers a toolbox, a bottle of gas, and a sextant, which "was the first thing he'd seen in a long time that stirred him" (192). In the end, the man is able to collect may useful items to bring back to his son.

They hurry to make dinner, and the father asks for the pistol. The boy realizes he has left it behind and begins to cry. They lose valuable daylight going to recover the pistol, which they find lying on the sand. When they return to the main path, night has fallen. Using lightning bolts, they find their old tracks and are able to find their old piece of tarp for shelter.

The next day, they spend the morning unloading goods from the ship. The father's cough continues to worsen; he coughs up blood often. "Every day is a lie, he said. But you are dying. That is not a lie" (200). The man finds a flare pistol from the ship and a first aid kit. The son learns that the man has kept the flare pistol to shoot people, not to signal, because there is no one to signal. The boy wants to shoot it that night as a celebration.

The boy asks whether the people who owned the ship are dead or alive. The man insists they could be alive, but this idea concerns the boy, who does not want to steal from others. In the end, the man agrees that they are most likely dead. On the beach, the boy suggests writing a message in the sand for the good guys, but the man mentions that the bad guys might see it. This discourages the boy. The man says they could still write a letter. They decide not to do so.

In the sand, the boy maps out a grid of streets. "The man walked down and squatted and looked at it. The boy looked up. The ocean's going to get it, isn't it? he said" (206). The man responds in the affirmative.

At night, they shoot the flare. The boy wonders who might be able to see the flare. When his father suggests God, he replies, "Yeah. Maybe somebody like that" (207).

The boy becomes ill and vomits. The father gives him expired antibiotics from the ship's first aid kit. The boy remains sick for some time, and the father's health gets no better.

Analysis

The one inevitable conclusion is death. While everything humans do and hope for could be seen as a kind of lie, an attempt to thwart death and make something lasting or at least something meaningful, the truth is that man is mortal. Thus the imagery of death in nature becomes more prominent in this section. Though the man and the boy have reached the ocean as they hoped, neither they nor the reader feels fulfilled by their accomplishment. The wasteland of death only continues at the coastline. "The bones of seabirds. At the tide line a woven mat of weeds and the ribs of fishes in their millions stretching along the shore as far as eye could see like an isocline [parallel pattern] of death. One vast salt sepulchre. Senseless. Senseless" (187). The repetition of "senseless" here emphasizes the indifference of the universe to death, even while mankind is all too keenly aware of and dismayed by it. At the sea, the man's health does not improve, and the boy becomes ill.

The short exchange about the ocean destroying the artificial streets carved into the sand is a metaphor for this broad theme in the novel: the infinite universe will eventually destroy man's constructions, whether through indifference or the insensible onslaught of the atrophies of time. The boy's mapping out of streets represents manmade phenomena like the civilization that is now destroyed. Meanwhile, the ocean, part of nature and the natural universe, will eventually obliterate the boy's map.

The name of the abandoned ship, *Bird of Hope*, is paradoxical. At face value, the ship does provide hope. Like some of the buildings along the way, it offers them many useful supplies to sustain them in the days to come. Yet, it seems that time and the sea have destroyed much else that would have been useful; the ship merely offers remnants. Besides, the *Bird of Hope* has ended up abandoned and stuck ashore. It did not complete its original mission and has been left for scavengers.

The sextant, which the father finds in the ship, is described as "the first thing he'd seen in a long time that stirred him" (192). A sextant helps people determine their position in relation to the celestial objects. In other words, the sextant is an invention of man that enables him to look up into the universe, to seek something higher, something beyond the earth upon which he lives, and locate himself in that context. Taking this into account, the sextant could be construed as a metaphor for hope.

The flare, too, symbolizes hope in a divine or celestial context. The boy wants to shoot it in celebration, not save it to shoot one of the bad guys. Maybe God will be the kind of being who sees it, since there are few people around to communicate with, and pretty much all of them seem to be the bad guys. Nevertheless, the boy in particular maintains a hope of human fellowship with the good guys. If the flare won't be seen, maybe a message in the sand will do. Yet, communication tends to be irreducibly ambiguous and can reach the bad guys as easily as the good guys, so the man and boy decide not even to write a letter.

Notably, darkness is personified in this section. When the boy and the man hurry to find their campsite before night falls, the boy asks, "Is the dark going to catch us?" (196). Unfortunately, it does. Like death in a previous section, the darkness is described as a human stalker, chasing the man and the boy across the road in search of shelter and safety. The flare, usually intended as a sign of distress, just lets the darkness know where to find them. They have to rely on the brief bursts of lightning, representing only momentary flashes of hope or solace, to get where they are going.

Summary and Analysis of Section 9

Section 9 goes from page 211 to page 231.

The man agonizes over his son's illness. He sleeps restlessly. Eventually when he awakens, the boy is better and his fever has broken. A couple of days later, the man and the boy continue to finesse their beach campsite. One day, the man sees prints in the sand as they return to their camp. They hurry back to their belongings, which have been completely ransacked.

The father decides to hunt down the robbers, so they track the prints. They find the thief pushing their cart and wielding a butcher's knife. The man aims the pistol at the thief. "He was an outcast from one of the communes and the fingers of his right hand had been cut away" (215). The man cocks his pistol and warns the thief to step away from their cart. The boy begs his father not to kill the thief. Accordingly, the father instead forces the thief to take off all of his clothes and put them in the cart.

The man leaves the thief naked on the side of the road. "I'm going to leave you the way you left us" (217). The boy cries and continues to look back at the thief as they return to their camp. The man tells him to stop crying. Nonetheless, the boy insists that they could still save the thief, who "was just hungry, Papa. He's going to die" (218). When the man points out that his son is not the one who must worry about the danger, the boy replies, "Yes I am, he said. I am the one" (218).

They return to the road where they left the thief and call out to him. They hear no answer, and they spend some time searching for him. Finally, the man simply leaves the thief's clothes and shoes in the road. Back at the camp, the father assures his son that he did not intend to kill the thief. The boy responds, "But we did kill him" (219).

They continue on their journey, and their health worsens. They find little along the way to help them. At the edge of one town, they are suddenly attacked with arrows by a man hiding in a building. The father is hit in the leg, but he manages to shoot the flare pistol at the building and set it on fire. The man tells the boy to remain with the cart in hiding, while he enters the house with the reloaded flare pistol.

Inside the house, the man sees a woman holding the arrow man. It is unclear whether he is dead or alive. She curses the father as he explores the house and searches for the bow, to no avail. Finding nothing, he leaves the house and departs with his son and their cart. They make camp at a store in the town. The man treats his wounded leg with the first aid kit. The man snaps at the boy when he does not respond quickly to the order to retrieve the first aid kit, but he later apologizes for yelling.

Ever since they left the thief naked, the boy has been quieter than usual. Cooped up in the store, the man tells the son that they must talk to each other. He offers to tell his son a story, but the boy rejects him. "Those stories are not true.... In the stories we're always helping people and we don't help people" (225). The father says that the son should tell him a story, or even a dream of his, but the boy replies that his stories are more "like real life" (227), unlike his father's stories. The boy thinks it only "okay" that they have survived many dark experiences.

Later, the man says aloud that he thinks their story of survival is pretty good. His son still does not want to talk, but he asks his father whether his father killed the arrow man. His father says no, reassuring him that this is the truth despite remaining privately unsure.

They leave the town two days later. During their journey, the man removes the stitches from his leg. During the nights, the man continues to dream of "human love, the songs of birds, the sun" (229). He grows steadily sicker as they plod forward. They pass by abandoned cars with corpses inside. As they walk, the man coughs up increasing amounts of blood. Among the items left on the road they find a canvas bag and a suitcase, which they take with them. The man must stop to rest on an old couch by the road.

Analysis

The incident with the thief presents a major conflict in *The Road.* At first it is a conflict between the protagonists and the thief, but it soon brings back the primary conflict between the protagonists. The thief's actions lead the man to punish the thief in a manner that the boy finds not only inappropriate but deathly wrong. Even though the man later agrees to return to help the thief, the thief has disappeared, and the boy says, " we did kill him" (219). Once the thief no longer has the knife, the boy responds to the thief in a way similar to how he responded to others they encountered. This incident further underscores the fundamental differences in outlook between the man and the boy with respect to how they treat others. The son wants to help as much as they can, and not to kill others, while the father is rightly suspicious of others and is willing to punish infractions with death or what amounts to death.

The scene with the arrow man continues the same theme. Given the son's empathy, the father does not want to suggest that he has killed yet another person. Thus he makes use of his superior position to resolve the ambiguity of whether the arrow man died, asking his son to trust him that the arrow man did not die.

This section also features an oft-quoted passage that alludes to the power of storytelling and human narrative. "At a crossroads a ground set with dolmen stones where the spoken bones of oracles lay moldering.... What will you say? A living man spoke these lines? He sharpened a quill with his small pen knife to scribe these things in sloe or lampblack? At some reckonable and entabled moment? He is coming to steal my eyes. To seal my mouth with dirt" (220). The first part of the passage relates to the oral tradition of humans, their storytelling ("living man spoke") and to their literate storytelling as well (literature and narrative written with a quill)

However, the one who comes to steal the man's eyes or to seal his mouth with dirt is preventing human communication, getting in the way of seeing others' writing and getting in the way of speaking. It appears that the so-called living man is the same one who returns to destroy communication. This perhaps alludes to death. In death, the man will be unable to narrate his own story and to validate the reality of his existence, and whatever he wrote comes to nothing. Or perhaps the storyteller, by carving specific lines, freezes his story at a time and place in a way that makes it impossible for the next person to speak or see something different. Either way, it seems to the narrator that the living man wrote the lines for himself and his time, not for the ones whose mouths will be sealed with dirt. It is a cynical, dejected view of storytelling that probably fits the protagonist father's present worldview. The father's stories are no longer of interest even to his son, who realizes that the stories of helping others do not match reality.

The nature imagery in one passage emphasizes the inevitability of death in the universal sweep. "Perhaps in the world's destruction it would be possible at last to see how it was made. Oceans, mountains. The ponderous counterspectacle of things ceasing to be. The sweeping waste, hydroptic and coldly secular. The silence" (231). Nature, "coldly secular," again indifferently proceeds without concern for man and his problems. Since the world's "destruction" correlates with "how it was made," we see an infinite expanse of indifference in the universe's existence. Death is present at both the inception and conclusion of the universe; it is strange and anachronistic that life somehow exists in the middle.

The man's worsening health and his leg wound point to the inevitable conclusion that his own death is near. One sentence in particular foreshadows how quickly his death is approaching. The man looks at his son, "[s]tanding with his suitcase like an orphan waiting for a bus" (231). In only a few days, the boy will indeed be an orphan. He will be standing on the side of the road, where he will be found by the man with a shotgun who "picks him up" (like a bus).

Summary and Analysis of Section 10

Section 10 begins at page 232 and ends at the end of the novel.

After two more days of travel, the protagonists arrive at a broad river with a collapsed bridge. The man says oddly, "What are we going to do Papa?" The boy answers, "Well what are we" (232). They raise a tarp for shelter, and the boy falls asleep. In the morning, they begin to walk inland, the man's cough worsening continuously. Finally, they reach a cleared area in the woods by a stream. "Here they camped and when he lay down he knew that he could go no further and that this was the place where he would die" (233).

The man is bedridden. He refuses to eat his share of a can of a fruit, but the boy insists on saving his father's half for the next day. The boy tries to make a tent, but his father does not want to be covered. The man wishes to be able to see, to watch his son sit by the fire. While the boy investigates their surroundings, the man remains at the camp. When the boy returns, his father begs him to continue the journey with the pistol.

The boy refuses to leave without his father. The man assures the boy that he knows how to carry the fire, that the fire is real inside of the boy. The boy reminds his father that he promised never to leave him. The man promises his son that he can still always talk to his father, even if they are not physically together. "You have to make it like talk that you imagine. And you'll hear me. You have to practice" (235).

The child travels down the road but then returns to his father, who sleeps. The boy talks to him and tries to listen for a response, then tries again. The father wakes up, still coughing. The boy asks his father if he remembers the little boy, and the man assures his son that the little boy was not lost. "Goodness will find the little boy. It always has. It will again" (236).

During the night, the boy holds his father. When the boy wakes up, his father is dead. The boy weeps, goes to the road, then returns to his father's side to hold his hand, crying his name. The boy remains by his father for three days. Finally, he returns to the road. He notices that someone is approaching. The boy stands by the road with the pistol in his hand. He has piled blankets over the man's body.

A man with a shotgun approaches the boy and asks him about his father. The boy tells him that his father has died, and the man tells the boy to join him. The boy asks whether the man is one of the good guys. The man says yes and tells the boy to put away his pistol. The man asks the boy to show him his father's body, but the boy is unresponsive. The man reveals that he is with a larger group of people who have known about the man and the boy. They apparently discussed whether or not to check on the boy. The man adds that the boy must take a chance with them or else die with his father.

The boy asks him whether he also carries the fire, but the man does not understand. When asked a second time, however, he responds that he is indeed carrying the fire. The man reveals that he has two children (a boy and a girl) and a wife. He promises the boy that they are not cannibals. The boy decides to join the man and his family.

The man checks the father's body and then tells the boy to go stand by the road. He will follow with the boy's belongings and the blankets. The boy does not want to leave his father or want people to see him, and he asks whether they can cover the body with one of the blankets. The man says yes.

When the man joins the boy, the boy tries to hand him the pistol but is told to keep it for himself. The boy asks to say goodbye to his papa, so he returns to the woods. "He cried for a long time. I'll talk to you every day, he whispered. And I wont forget. No matter what" (241).

The wife of the man, upon their arrival, hugs the boy. She tries to talk to the boy about God sometimes, but the boy finds it easier to talk to his father. "The woman said that was all right. She said that the breath of God was his breath yet though it pass from man to man through all of time" (241).

The Road ends with a short paragraph describing trout swimming in a stream from a distant time. "On their backs were vermiculate patterns that were maps of the world in its becoming. Maps and mazes. Of a thing which could not be put back. Not be made right again. In the deep glens where they lived all things were older than man and they hummed of mystery" (241).

Analysis

At the time of his death, the father reassures the son that they can still talk to one another and that the son will be able to hear him. "If I'm not here you can still talk to me. You can talk to me and I'll talk to you. You'll see" (235). Later, the boy does choose to talk to his father instead of talking to God. The woman agrees that this alternative is acceptable, saying "that the breath of God was his breath yet though it pass from man to man through all of time" (241). This could be her acceptance of secular prayer, an alternative form of spirituality, but it more likely is her acknowledgment of the divine fire within human beings that connects them to God.

These alternatives express the ultimate, metaphysical conflict in the novel. Is the universe really so indifferent, as the whole environment has seemed, or is there something irreducibly divine in the human spirit, a fire that really does make people "good guys" if they choose to be? Is life a weird anachronism in the universe's expanse of indifferent death, or are human life, compassion, and hope impossible to ignore as real phenomena within the universe?

On the eve of the man's death, the boy and the man discuss the little boy from Section 3. The son remains concerned that the little boy is lost, and we wonder if he is thinking about himself. He is soon to be in the boy's position, with nobody looking after him, being "the one" to whom it falls to make moral decisions and choices where life and death are at stake. The son wants to know who will find the little boy, which suggests a similar concern about himself after the man's death. When the man reassures his son that goodness will find the little boy, it is hopeful foreshadowing: "It always has. It will again" (236). While there seems to be little chance of this result, indeed some rare "good guys" find the son and rescue him. This preservation of the son into the next scene, into the next generation, suggests the hopeful alternative for human civilization rather than the one that characterized the father's generation of death and destruction, of the seeming total indifference of the world.

The Road's denouement is thus a rescue. It is the redeeming act that the father seems to have been looking for. The journey, at least from the father's point of view, was to ensure his son's survival. He suggested that it was mission appointed by God in order that the boy be protected. Finally, at the conclusion of the novel, it appears that this goal has been achieved. The boy now has a family again and some kind of home, and he is presumably going to be relatively safe once again, perhaps no longer to wander the road.

The trout, described in the last passage of *The Road*, recall an earlier mention of trout near the beginning of the novel: "Where once he'd watched trout swaying in the current, tracing their perfect shadows on the stones beneath" (25). At the conclusion of the novel, the trout are described as having backs with "patterns that were maps of the world in its becoming. Maps and mazes. Of a thing which could not be put back. Not be made right again" (241). This vivid imagery suggests that the trout bear some significance in the novel, encoding the unfolding and refolding of life and civilization in the world, bearing the mark of the universe's inevitable playing out of first principles. The secrets ("maps and mazes") of the world from its inception ("in its becoming") are retained by these trout, which are the present's incarnation of the first principles in action. Furthermore, these secrets "could not be put back"—like Prometheus' fire or Pandora's box, the laws of the cosmos will continue to unfold. Indifference, violence, hope, whatever emerges in the universe will play itself out and will not "be made right again." If human civilization inevitably leads to its own destruction, the basic patterns of humanity will last so long as there are humans, and the basic patterns of the universe, mapped on the trout, will last so long as the universe lasts.

Finally, the man and the boy remain noticeably unnamed in *The Road*, as do almost all of the other characters. This lack of naming, which prevents the reader from pinpointing the novel's setting "[a]t some reckonable and entabled moment," lifts the status of the protagonists' story to that of a parable, rather than just another post-apocalyptic tale. The man and the boy could be any father and son who carry the hope of basic humanity. Through the character of the boy in particular, McCarthy demonstrates the power of human resilience in the face of the universe's seeming indifference. Despite the human capacity for violence, the boy survives as one of the "good guys" and manages to carry the fire. This fire refers to the human capacities for hope and love. These capacities protect mankind from itself and suggest that the universe might not be totally indifferent after all. If the boy will be able to take part in a new construction of civilization, he may learn whether despite everything, goodness will continue to find its way.

Suggested Essay Questions

1. **How does the man demonstrate his love for his son in *The Road*?**

   The man demonstrates consistently that he is prepared to take whatever action necessary, even if violent, to ensure his son's survival and best interests. The most obvious example of this occurs when the man does not hesitate to shoot the attacker who holds a knife to the boy's throat. In less dramatic examples, the man continually sacrifices his own health to give his son nourishment. He also works hard to reassure his son that they are good people who hold the fire of goodness within them, and that they would never do things like eat other humans.
2. **Overall, does *The Road* put forth a positive and uplifting view of humanity, or one of darkness and pessimism?**

   The striking last paragraph, with its vivid imagery of trout hidden in deep mountain glens, offers a redemptive ending to what has been a story of awful indifference and destruction, where hope has eked out a meager, slight existence in the face of the ubiquitous destructiveness of human nature, which has both caused the catastrophe and perpetuated the evils in the world afterward. The boy's rescue by a family of "good guys" might be read as an ironic ending with hope in the face of disaster, where somehow the good-guy fire persists. The result is optimistic resilience, a hope against hope, which offers humans an existential choice about how they want to live, whether or not human nature and physical nature make those choices easy or hard.
3. **How do the man and the man's wife differ in their conceptions of death?**

   Both the man and his wife understand that in this post-apocalyptic environment, they are likely to be brutalized at the hands of rapists, murderers, and cannibals. The wife considers death to be a needed relief from these threats. To the contrary, the father considers death an abhorrent threat that would prevent him from protecting his son; his commitment to life drives him on the journey south to ensure his son's survival.
4. **Discuss at least two contrasting ways in which the survivors of the catastrophe deal with the chaos.**

   The man's wife responds to the catastrophic circumstances by committing suicide and avoiding whatever gruesome fate might befall her. Scavengers on the road choose to resort to murder, thievery, and cannibalism in order to survive. For them, humanity, kindness, and empathy are greatly diminished, it seems, although many of them continue to live in groups. The man and the boy, however, choose to scavenge and refrain from harming others unless violence is absolutely necessary to their survival.

5. **What is the significance of "the fire" to the man and the boy?**

That the man and the boy internally "carry the fire" signifies that they are the "good guys." Upon his deathbed, the man assures the boy that the fire can be found within the boy. The fire represents internal human strength in the form of qualities such as hope, perseverance and resilience, as well as morality, the ability to retain one's humanity in the face of ultimate destruction and evil.

6. **How do the protagonists distinguish the "good guys" from the "bad guys"? Are the protagonists indeed the "good guys"?**

The man and the boy consider themselves good guys, which they tend to see as seeking survival without harming others. They only scavenge for food and supplies, but they try not to steal from others, and they punish those who steal from them. In contrast, the "bad guys" are willing to hurt, use, or murder others for their own benefit. Yet, a central conflict in the novel is between the boy's idea of what good guys do, on the one hand, and what the father does, on the other hand, in being so afraid of others that he refuses to help them, and in more severely punishing others than the boy thinks is necessary.

7. **How does the boy's relationship with his father change over the course of their journey?**

The boy matures over the course of this journey, and his changing relationship with his father reflects this growing maturity. At the beginning of the novel, the boy looks to the father for knowledge and guidance, believing his father to speak the truth unequivocally. However, as he gains new experiences, the boy learns to use his own judgment and can assess somewhat better whether or not his father is telling the truth. He begins to question his father's honesty on such matters as whether or not they are truly the "good guys" and asserts his own opinion when believing that they should help other people. He never doubts his father's love for him, however, and continues to love and trust his father, even while he begins to have more and more serious reservations about his father's choices. In a sense, it is time for the father to die when the son is mature enough to make his own moral decisions for the new generation.

8. **What purpose do the father's memories and dreams serve in *The Road*?**

The man's recurring memories and dreams poignantly underscore, often by contrast with, the hopeless destruction and chaotic violence which characterize his situation in reality. These passages also demonstrate the man's struggle not to succumb to wishful fantasies but instead to persevere throughout the journey's seemingly insurmountable hardships. The vivid excerpts from his past life remind him (and the reader) that such a life did once exist, despite the hellish present circumstances.

9. **Discuss some of the literary techniques used by McCarthy to evoke and maintain the novel's largely grim and bleak setting.**

   Perhaps the most important literary devices used to achieve this end are flashbacks, repetition, and vivid imagery of nature. The bleak imagery he evokes insistently impress upon the reader the extremely harsh conditions the protagonists must face. Throughout the novel, the boy and the man also touch upon the same themes in their conversations: whether they will die of starvation; being the good guys; carrying the fire. These repetitions or mantras keep the sobering themes of death, violence, and unlikely survival to the fore. Furthermore, the contrasting flashbacks, full of life and color, juxtaposed with the imagery of a dead land inhabited by the walking dead, highlight the gravity of the protagonists' present circumstances. The flashbacks also scramble the linear telling of the story, seeming to lengthen the arduous journey endured by the man and the boy.

10. **Describe the role of trust in the novel.**

    Trust or the lack of trust is the expression of a basic human relationship. Those who can be trusted will work together; those who cannot be trusted will be either ignored or killed. The father's paranoid and unsympathetic behavior towards other travelers on the road, though they may be harmless like Ely and the burnt man, stem from his distrust of all other individuals, because of his past experience. The boy has seen much less trouble in his short life and tends to trust others much more. His trust in his father reflects his love but also his immaturity, and as he matures he learns to decipher the situations in which his father may be lying to protect him, so that by the end of the novel, he does not simply take his father's words at face value.

McCarthy, Genre, and Violence

Despite McCarthy's unique prose style, diction, and other choices, many readers and critics strive to pigeonhole his works into particular genres. They often disagree on the subject of the reclusive author's intent and style, with much discussion over whether he is a Southern or a Western writer, whether his works are modern or postmodern, or whether any of his Westerns are truly part of the genre at all. For example, the *Border Trilogy* and *Blood Meridian* are sometimes called Westerns, but these works obliterate many of the traditional tropes of the genre. Likewise, *The Road* has been classified rather narrowly as a science fiction novel or horror novel, but neither category fits well. It does not help to say that *The Road* is a drama, though it certainly is more of a tragedy than a comedy.

McCarthy's unrelentingly honest and unglorified depictions of violence and human cruelty in his novels, such as in *Blood Meridian* and *The Road*, strike readers deeply. Their violence defies categorization. Unlike traditional Westerns, for instance, the violence of the "bad guys" comes out of severe desperation. Morality has all but broken down, and we are not really sure how good the "good guys" are, while the "bad guys" might easily argue that they have no choice if they want to survive.

If [The Road] fits any genre, it is in the class of post-apocalyptic novels like *Left Behind*, which is the title of one of the *New York Times* book reviews. This is no Christian novel, however, except in its Calvinistic austerity and suggestions of the root evil of human nature apart from divinity. To be sure, the man's (debatable) belief in God may propel him forward to ensure his son's survival, even in times of despair and isolation. Ultimately, however, his faith cannot explain what has happened to civilization and does not save his son. Only the man's heroic actions, which are by no means divine or divinely influenced, save his son. His internal "fire" is indeed redemptive, but it is no Holy Spirit at work. After the man's death, his son finds it easier to talk to his dead father than to God. The boy is told, "the breath of God was his breath yet though it pass from man to man through all of time" (241). Man through all of time, however, has led to the post-apocalyptic present. Even the godspoke men, having destroyed the earth and themselves, are gone. Those who remain in this wasteland of primitive life return to marauding, murder, and cannibalism.

Perhaps the terror experienced by the man and the boy on the road has less to do with the horrifying atrocities they witness, and more to do with the realization that such acts committed by humans are timeless, universal, inevitable. In the universal sweep, humans are a strange blip of life and loss. The unsettling serenity and indifference of the universe, in which humans existentially find themselves, makes the tale a terrifying mix of theological angst and humanistic hope. These are characters who truly are working out their salvation with Kierkegaard's infinite resignation, and with fear and trembling.

Author of ClassicNote and Sources

D. Dona Le, author of ClassicNote. Completed on July 24, 2009, copyright held by GradeSaver.

Updated and revised Adam Kissel September 19, 2009. Copyright held by GradeSaver.

McCarthy, Cormac. The Road. London: Picador, 2006.

McCarthy, Cormac. No Country for Old Men. London: Picador, 2007.

White, J.M. "The Road (Book Review)." Appalachian Heritage. 2006-12-01. 2009-07-20. <http://74.125.155.132/search?q=cache%3ALkkXX4qZdvMJ%3Acommunity.berea.edu%2F

Whitmer, Benjamin. "The Road (Book Review)." The Modern Word. 2006-10-23. 2009-07-18. <http://www.themodernword.com/reviews/mccarthy_road.html>.

Woodward, Richard B. "Cormac McCarthy's Venomous Fiction." The New York Times. 1992-04-19. 2009-07-14. <http://www.nytimes.com/books/98/05/17/specials/mccarthy-venom.html?_r=3>.

Kollin, Susan. "Genre and the Geographies of Violence: Cormac McCarthy and the Contemporary Western." *Contemporary Literature* 42:3 (Autumn 2001): 557-588. JSTOR. TCD Libraries, Dublin, Ireland. 18 July 2009. <http://www.jstor.org/stable/1208996>.

Ellis, Jay. "'What Happens to Country' in *Blood Meridian.*" *Rocky Mountain Review of Language and Literature* 60:1 (2006): 85-97. JSTOR. TCD Libraries, Dublin, Ireland. 18 July 2009. <http://www.jstor.org/stable/4143880>.

Essay: Carrying the Fire: Effective Literary Devices in McCarthy's The Road

by Megan Elizabeth Farris
December 05, 2007

Cormac McCarthy's novel The Road is a gripping tale of survival in a post-nuclear holocaust world full of marauders and cannibals. A man and his son travel the United States in search of food and shelter, all the while hiding from (and occasionally battling) the marauders. As one might expect, the novel is very dark. The situation for the man and boy is hopeless, and McCarthy uses a great deal of devices to efficiently portray the desperate journey of his two protagonists.

An interesting device McCarthy uses is the lack of names or physical descriptions of the man and boy, aside from the boy calling his father "Papa." McCarthy provides no physical descriptions or ages except when the father describes the boy as thin. The two use no regional dialect when speaking, and no exact description of their location appears. The back cover of the novel says that it takes place in America, but McCarthy never even gives this broad detail within the story. All the reader knows is a broad sketch of their travels: from mountains to coast, and from north to south. One might assume that the two are at first somewhere in the Appalachian Mountains, heading southeast to the east coast of the United States. The author, however, takes care never to reveal definitive locations. All of this lack of description of both the people and their location gives the novel a sense of anonymity – a sense that if such a nuclear holocaust were to happen, these two suffering people could be anyone. All people need the basic essentials in the face of such an apocalypse, and previous identities are meaningless.

Another important device McCarthy uses is sentence fragments and lack of proper punctuation. Sentence fragments occur early in the novel and continue throughout. Often, sentence fragments extend from a single short sentence, as if they should be connected with commas, such as "In the dream from which he'd wakened he had wandered in a cave where the child led him by the hand. Their light playing over the wet flowstone walls. Like pilgrims in a fable swallowed up and lost among the inward parts of some gigantic beast" (McCarthy 3). Later, McCarthy writes, "Standing there he felt the hull of the ship lift and slide. Just slightly. Tide coming in. Slapping along the rocks of the jetty down there" (228). These are just two examples of sentence fragments that are used throughout the novel. The author uses fragments to illustrate the figurative fragmentation of the world in which the man and boy live.

Proper punctuation also occurs infrequently in The Road. Quotation marks are never used in dialogue, and contractions often lack apostrophes, such as in "Cant you, Papa?" (7). Apostrophes are used in contractions, but are just as frequently not used, and their usage doesn't seem to form any pattern. The author seems to be using the lack of punctuation and proper sentence structure to show the futility of all the rules of the English language. In a world where nothing matters but finding food, shelter and clothing, punctuation and sentence structure do not matter. Along with comments about material possessions such as cars and electronics being left roadside because they are useless, McCarthy uses these language errors to show that all of society's conventions and cares are worthless.

Last but not least, McCarthy uses religious language and references to light throughout the novel when writing about the boy. The child is referred to as "God's own firedrake" (31) early in the novel, and Biblical references to the child continue as the novel progresses. Later, when the father and son meet a man named Ely on the road, the two adults have an interesting conversation about the child:

"When I saw that boy I thought that I had died. [Ely]

You thought he was an angel? [Father]

I didnt know what he was. I never thought to see a child again. I didnt know that would happen. [Ely]

What if I said that he's a god?" [Father] (172).

This apparent deification of the child is developed even more before and after this section. At one point, the father plays with his son's hair as he sleeps, thinking to himself, "Golden chalice, good to house a god" (75). He begins referring to the child as Christ or God later in the story. He does not ever directly say that the boy is God, but the author always follows the man's references to God with a glance at the boy, or a touch. For example, McCarthy writes, "Christ, he said. Oh Christ. He turned and grabbed the boy" (110), then goes on to say, "Christ, he said. Run. Run" (111). Not only does he speak to the boy as if he were Christ, but the boy eventually begins to answer to this. When they find the bomb shelter full of food, McCarthy writes

"Oh my God, he whispered. Oh my God.

What is it Papa?

Come down. Oh my God. Come down." (138).

It seems as though the father is addressing the son as God, with the child answering. This type of dialogue occurs again on page 253. If these Biblical addresses aren't convincing enough, the boy actually says, following his father's statement that he is not the one who has to worry about their situation, "Yes, I am… I am the one" (259). This short statement brings to mind Jesus' Biblical affirmation that he is "the way, the truth, and the life."

The boy is also associated strongly with light. In Revelation 21:5, it says, "They will need no light or lamps from the sun, for the Lord God shall give them light." The man constantly tells his son that they are "carrying the fire," something which provides light for their dark world. The father, on his deathbed, watches his son and thinks to himself, "There was light all about him… when he moved the light moved with him" (277). The boy's strong ties to divinity seem to be used to shed some form of hope and light on his novel of darkness, reinforced by the ending in which a seeming miracle occurs – the boy finds other people who are "carrying the light" after his father dies.

McCarthy's novel The Road is full of hopelessness and danger. The author uses anonymity, lack of sentence structure, and incorrect punctuation to demonstrate this sense of despair. On the other hand, he effectively uses Christ-like references to the boy to show a vague sense of innate good in the world – or perhaps simply desperate hope – even in the face of an apocalypse.

Essay: The Road from Coorain

by Anahita Amalsad
February 25, 2007

The Road from Coorain

In Conway's novel, The Road from Coorain, she explains that both of her parents had great determination to succeed in their endeavors. Conway's mother, Eve, and father, Bill, influenced their children's life paths and choices, especially in the case of Jill, in numerous ways. Conway had a rather rocky relationship with her mother, in that there were many highs and lows. Her mother pushed her to study hard; however, when she fell sick, Conway had to take care of her mother, which led to some resentment and changes in her career plans. Although Conway's parents are indirect characters to this novel, their determination and relationship to Conway plays a large role in her life, helping to shape her character and choices in numerous ways.

Conway's mother proved from the start to be a very determined woman in many different areas. Growing up, she fell under the category where "daughters were expected to wait on males and to defer to the judgment of the older sons." She faced gender prejudice in many areas, starting as a child when she "began to work in an office...[only to have her] earnings [go] to support [her] unemployed older brothers." Moreover, when it came to education, Eve felt strongly about it from childhood. As a child, she self taught herself, and worked her way up to a successful nurse. This determination that Jill's mother emits is definitely a characteristic that was passed on to her children. Jill's determination can be seen in many areas, one of which is in her education. Eve's drive towards education eventually rubs off on Jill, and she starts taking school seriously, and in turn does extremely well. However, she faces the same hardship her mother faced in that there is great prejudice against women in the society.

This prejudice against gender proves to be a continuous problem for Jill and her mother throughout the novel. With the death of Jill's father, Eve endured great pressure to sell Coorain. She did not receive the encouragement she needed from others to run Coorain; instead, she was constantly told to sell Coorain because a woman could not do a good job of running it. However, through her determination and perseverance she stayed strong and ran Coorain well, until the death of her son. Even then, when her health and sanity started to fail, she "[hired] a manager to take care of [Coorain]" rather than selling it. Jill, too, endured the painful deaths of her father and brother, yet remained strong and determined in her endeavors.

It is clear that Jill's mother had a profound influence on her life. With the deterioration of her mother's health, after the death of Bill and Bob, it was Jill that she leaned on for support. Their strong mother daughter relationship slowly depleted with Jill's mother's new sense of overprotection and attachment towards Jill. Seeing her mother sick affected Jill negatively, because she had to take off from school to take care of her mother. However, although she struggled, the persistence she acquired from her mother led her back to school, where she graduated with the highest of honors. Like her mother, it took a great setback to cause Jill to become depressed. Staying strong through the deaths of her family member, she eventually fell hard when she was not accepted for a prestigious traineeship with the Department of External Affairs solely because she was a woman. Jill states, "I could scarcely believe that my refusal was because I was a woman." This caused a sense of helplessness to fill her soul; however, she continued to try, and later decided to move to California with the determination to better herself.

Although not mentioned as much as Eve, Jill's father played an important role in Jill's life as well. Jill obtains a strong bond with her father from early on because she works as her father's apprentice from young age of eight years old. Her father teaches her to undergo the intense labor of sheep herding, which teaches her determination and perseverance. One can see Bill's kind, charismatic, and passionate nature, because he is determined to make a kingdom for his wife and children. He is also a very unwavering character because he secured the sprawling, remote pastoral station. However, it is implied that because he is unable to overcome the drought that takes over Coorain, he drowns himself when he goes to fix a livestock pond. Bill's death is one of many hardships Jill must endure, and it takes a toll on her emotions because of that strong father daughter bond. Even at the end, Jill mentions that she can hear her father's voice echoing in her ears, portraying that no matter how much time has passed, the early teachings of her father, coupled with his memories, will remain with her forever.

Jill Conway's parents, Eve and Bill, both had great determination to succeed in their endeavors. Both of her parents greatly influenced her life path and choices in positive ways by teaching her perseverance. Conway's relationship with her father was the bond that they created when she was a little girl. The relationship with her mother was filled with ups and downs, in that it went from a solid relationship, to one where Jill wanted to escape. Although her father was a very determined man, he could not take the pressure placed upon him, thus committing suicide. Her mom, too, fell into depression after the deaths of her husband and son. Jill on the other hand learned positive aspects from her parents, but bettered herself in end by not following in their footsteps. Instead of falling apart due to heartbreak and depressing times, Jill decided to start new by leaving Sydney and moving to California, determined to create a better life and future for herself.

Quiz 1

1. **What was McCarthy's given name at birth?**
   A. Cormac McCarthy
   B. Cullen McCarthy
   C. Charles McCarthy
   D. John McCarthy

2. **Which of the following works does not belong in the Border Trilogy?**
   A. All the Pretty Horses
   B. Suttree
   C. Cities of the Plain
   D. The Crossing

3. **Which of the following works has not been adapted to film?**
   A. No Country for Old Men
   B. All the Pretty Horses
   C. The Road
   D. Child of God

4. **For which novel was McCarthy awarded a Pulitzer Prize?**
   A. The Road
   B. Blood Meridian
   C. Suttree
   D. The Crossing

5. **Where was Cormac McCarthy born?**
   A. Ireland
   B. Tennessee
   C. Rhode Island
   D. Texas

6. **McCarthy's editor for I[The Orchard Keeper] was also the editor for which author?**
   A. Marcel Proust
   B. William Faulkner
   C. Ernest Hemingway
   D. Henry James

7. **The name "Cormac" means:**
   A. son of Charles
   B. Charles
   C. son of John
   D. John

8. **In which of the following genres have McCarthy's works NOT been seriously classified?**
   A. romance
   B. Western
   C. crime thriller
   D. science fiction

9. **To whom is The Road dedicated?**
   A. John Francis McCarthy
   B. Albert Erskine
   C. Cullen McCarthy
   D. Jennifer Winkley

10. **With whom did McCarthy give his first televised interview?**
   A. Oprah Winfrey
   B. Barbara Walters
   C. Larry King
   D. Bil O'Reilly

11. **At the beginning of the novel, what do the protagonists recover from the abandoned gas station?**
   A. nothing
   B. motor oil
   C. food
   D. a telephone

12. **In what direction are the father and son traveling?**
   A. east
   B. west
   C. north
   D. south

13. **What type of soda can does the man find and give to his son?**
   A. Sprite
   B. Coca Cola
   C. Tab
   D. Pepsi

14. **In what country are the man and his son traveling?**
   A. Mexico
   B. United States
   C. England
   D. Canada

15. **How is the man wounded when the protagonists are ambushed in an abandoned town?**
   A. He is shot by a gun.
   B. An arrow pierces his leg.
   C. He is stabbed.
   D. He is shot by a flare pistol.

16. **Where does the man leave his wife's photograph?**
   A. on the road
   B. in the ocean
   C. in the woods
   D. in his wallet

17. **Who does the man shoot in the head with the pistol?**
   A. the man from the truck
   B. the man with a shotgun
   C. the thief
   D. the pregnant woman

18. **During what time of the year does The Road take place?**
   A. winter-spring
   B. spring-summer
   C. fall-winter
   D. summer-fall

19. **What do the protagonists find underneath the steel-padlocked door?**
    A. bullets
    B. food
    C. fresh water
    D. naked humans

20. **What are the long-term goals of the man and the boy?**
    A. To leave the country.
    B. They do not know.
    C. To live at the sea.
    D. None.

21. **What is the supposed name of the man who spends one night with them?**
    A. Ely
    B. Evan
    C. Aaron
    D. Eliot

22. **What do they find still smoldering on a spit at a hastily abandoned camp?**
    A. a human infant
    B. a dog
    C. vegetables
    D. unidentified meat

23. **Translated into English, what is the name of the ship they find by the beach?**
    A. Bird of Hope
    B. Bird of Prey
    C. Angel of Hope
    D. Bird of Light

24. **What additional weapon do they find on the ship?**
    A. butcher knife
    B. automatic weapon
    C. rifle
    D. flare pistol

25. **How does the man punish the thief?**

A. he takes all of the thief's food

B. he takes all of the thief's clothing and shoes

C. he beats the thief

D. he kills the thief

Quiz 1 Answer Key

1. **(C)** Charles McCarthy
2. **(B)** Suttree
3. **(D)** Child of God
4. **(A)** The Road
5. **(C)** Rhode Island
6. **(B)** William Faulkner
7. **(A)** son of Charles
8. **(A)** romance
9. **(A)** John Francis McCarthy
10. **(A)** Oprah Winfrey
11. **(B)** motor oil
12. **(D)** south
13. **(B)** Coca Cola
14. **(B)** United States
15. **(B)** An arrow pierces his leg.
16. **(A)** on the road
17. **(A)** the man from the truck
18. **(C)** fall-winter
19. **(D)** naked humans
20. **(B)** They do not know.
21. **(A)** Ely
22. **(A)** a human infant
23. **(A)** Bird of Hope
24. **(D)** flare pistol
25. **(B)** he takes all of the thief's clothing and shoes

Quiz 2

1. **What does the boy pile on top of his father's body after his death?**
    A. leaves
    B. nothing
    C. blankets
    D. a tarp

2. **Which of the following is not a prominent theme in The Road?**
    A. paternal love
    B. romantic love
    C. survival/resilience
    D. death

3. **The "fire," mentioned multiple times throughout the novel by the boy and his father, does not refer to:**
    A. unquenchable humanity
    B. capacity for hope
    C. willingness to murder for food
    D. resilience

4. **Death is personified as:**
    A. a thief
    B. a lover
    C. a banker
    D. a doctor

5. **At the start of the novel, how many bullets are in the man's pistol?**
    A. 1
    B. 2
    C. 4
    D. 6

6. **The man fully loads the pistol with:**
    A. nothing
    B. fake whittled bullets
    C. bits of metal
    D. real bullets

7. **With what academic institution is Cormac McCarthy currently affiliated (as of 2009)?**
   A. University of Tennessee
   B. Santa Fe Institute
   C. University of Iowa
   D. Santa Fe Community College

8. **What weapon is carried by the man who rescues the boy after his father's death?**
   A. pistol
   B. shotgun
   C. none
   D. knife

9. **The woman whose family rescues the boy at the end of the novel talks to him about:**
   A. family
   B. school
   C. God
   D. girls

10. **The boy becomes upset with his father for various incidents throughout the novel, except for:**
    A. punishing the thief
    B. not stopping to help the burnt man
    C. not stopping to find the little boy
    D. not giving him enough food

11. **The novel concludes with a description of which of the following animals?**
    A. horses
    B. cows
    C. crows
    D. trout

12. **What body part is the thief missing?**
    A. his entire left hand
    B. his entire right hand
    C. fingers on his left hand
    D. fingers on his right hand

13. **What aspect of the ocean disappoints the boy?**
    A. the roughness
    B. the size
    C. the color
    D. the cleanliness

14. **After swimming in the ocean, what does the boy do?**
    A. He goes for a run.
    B. He becomes inexplicably happy.
    C. He becomes inexplicably upset.
    D. He fights with his father.

15. **How old does Ely pretend to be?**
    A. 40
    B. 60
    C. 80
    D. 90

16. **What instrument does the father make for his son?**
    A. violin
    B. clarinet
    C. recorder
    D. flute

17. **What does the boy do with the instrument his father gives him?**
    A. The boy throws it away.
    B. The boy keeps it.
    C. The boy breaks it.
    D. The boy buries it.

18. **What type of weather do the protagonists not experience?**
    A. tornado
    B. harsh wind
    C. rain
    D. snow

19. **The man and the boy do not explore a derelict:**
    A. ship
    B. gas station
    C. house
    D. condominium

20. **How old is the boy they encounter on the road?**
    A. 5
    B. 10
    C. 15
    D. unknown

21. **How do the protagonists interact with the burnt man?**
    A. They leave him behind.
    B. They give him clothes.
    C. They give him food.
    D. They give him medication.

22. **At one point in the novel, the man and the boy run into three armed men. What weapons do these men carry?**
    A. knives
    B. bows and arrows
    C. guns
    D. pipes

23. **What event has caused the destruction and chaos described in The Road?**
    A. unknown
    B. World War III
    C. nuclear war
    D. a natural disaster

24. **Complete the quote: "There is no God and we are his ____."**
    A. slaves
    B. prophets
    C. men
    D. followers

25. **How many children did Cormac McCarthy have with Anne DeLisle?**

A. one son

B. two sons

C. zero

D. one daughter

Quiz 2 Answer Key

1. **(C)** blankets
2. **(B)** romantic love
3. **(C)** willingness to murder for food
4. **(B)** a lover
5. **(B)** 2
6. **(B)** fake whittled bullets
7. **(B)** Santa Fe Institute
8. **(B)** shotgun
9. **(C)** God
10. **(D)** not giving him enough food
11. **(D)** trout
12. **(D)** fingers on his right hand
13. **(C)** the color
14. **(C)** He becomes inexplicably upset.
15. **(D)** 90
16. **(D)** flute
17. **(A)** The boy throws it away.
18. **(A)** tornado
19. **(D)** condominium
20. **(D)** unknown
21. **(A)** They leave him behind.
22. **(D)** pipes
23. **(A)** unknown
24. **(B)** prophets
25. **(C)** zero

Quiz 3

1. **The imagery of "the fire" perhaps relates to imagery used in which of the following McCarthy novels?**
   A. No Country for Old Men
   B. Blood Meridian
   C. Suttree
   D. The Crossing

2. **What does the man's wife believe will be his sole motivation to survive?**
   A. his exceptional physical strength
   B. his fear of starvation
   C. his fear of death
   D. their son

3. **What is the definition of "intestate"?**
   A. having died leaving behind a legitimately executed will
   B. relating to transportation between states
   C. having died without leaving behind a legitimately executed will
   D. having intestines

4. **The imagery regarding the fire evokes what figure in Greek mythology?**
   A. Apollo
   B. Zeus
   C. Prometheus
   D. Athena

5. **McCarthy's Border Trilogy is often considered to belong to what genre?**
   A. horror
   B. romance
   C. Western
   D. science fiction

6. **The violence depicted in McCarthy's works is usually not:**
   A. chaotic
   B. seemingly pointless
   C. glorified
   D. devoid of regenerative meaning

7. **At one point in the novel, McCarthy describes the land as "cauterized," which means:**
   A. flooded
   B. cold
   C. vast
   D. burnt

8. **By what means does the man's wife commit suicide?**
   A. pistol
   B. sharpened piece of obsidian
   C. hanging
   D. purposeful starvation

9. **Which of the following actions does the man not commit to demonstrate his love for and protectiveness of the boy?**
   A. He sews a new coat for the boy.
   B. He puts the boy's nutrition before his own.
   C. He gives the pistol to the boy whenever they are separated.
   D. He kills another human being to protect the boy.

10. **What are the father's dreams usually about?**
   A. the boy
   B. life before the catastrophe
   C. the catastrophe
   D. his prospective future

11. **What is the name of the university literary magazine in which McCarthy began his career?**
   A. The Independent
   B. The Sphinx
   C. The Phoenix
   D. The Journal

12. **What is a morel?**
   A. a type of poison
   B. a type of mushroom
   C. a type of bird
   D. a type of fish

13. **What does the boy dream about that deeply frightens him, when he describes the dream to his father?**
    A. falling trees
    B. the apocalypse
    C. wind-up penguin
    D. cannibals

14. **What animal do the protagonists hear but not see on the road, and only once?**
    A. a cat
    B. a dog
    C. a cow
    D. a crow

15. **What household object does the man use to conceal the latch door under which he and the boy hide?**
    A. television set
    B. mattress
    C. couch
    D. dining table

16. **During the journey, the man thinks of a long ago time when he watched a group of men set fire to what?**
    A. a house
    B. a forest
    C. a mass of serpents
    D. a pile of wood

17. **The man reassures his son that who or what will find the little boy, whom his son sees but is forbidden to help?**
    A. another family
    B. goodness
    C. cannibals
    D. evil

18. **Where does the man die?**
    A. in a clearing in the woods
    B. on the beach
    C. in the ocean
    D. in the desert

19. **At the beach, what valuable possession does the boy nearly lose?**
    A. his shoes
    B. the candle
    C. the pistol
    D. the lighter

20. **Why does the boy want to shoot the flare pistol at night?**
    A. to reveal their location
    B. to seek help
    C. to use up the flares
    D. to celebrate

21. **What object from the boat is "the first thing he'd seen in a long time that stirred him"?**
    A. a sextant
    B. maps
    C. cans of milk
    D. first-aid kit

22. **What do the man and the boy discover that hails from Tenerife?**
    A. a toolbox
    B. an abandoned ship
    C. a food label
    D. a suit jacket

23. **How many children does the man with a shotgun say he has?**
    A. 1
    B. 2
    C. 5
    D. none

24. **With which character do the protagonists have the most extensive contact?**
    A. burnt man
    B. Ely
    C. arrow man
    D. man with a shotgun

25. **Why are the naked people imprisoned?**

A. for hard labor

B. for their crimes

C. to be eaten

D. for body heat

Quiz 3 Answer Key

1. **(A)** No Country for Old Men
2. **(D)** their son
3. **(C)** having died without leaving behind a legitimately executed will
4. **(C)** Prometheus
5. **(C)** Western
6. **(C)** glorified
7. **(D)** burnt
8. **(B)** sharpened piece of obsidian
9. **(A)** He sews a new coat for the boy.
10. **(B)** life before the catastrophe
11. **(C)** The Phoenix
12. **(B)** a type of mushroom
13. **(C)** wind-up penguin
14. **(B)** a dog
15. **(B)** mattress
16. **(C)** a mass of serpents
17. **(B)** goodness
18. **(A)** in a clearing in the woods
19. **(C)** the pistol
20. **(D)** to celebrate
21. **(A)** a sextant
22. **(B)** an abandoned ship
23. **(B)** 2
24. **(B)** Ely
25. **(C)** to be eaten

Quiz 4

1. **How has the burnt man come to be thus injured, most likely?**
    A. unknown
    B. lightning
    C. barbecue accident
    D. forest fire

2. **Who directed the widely praised film No Country for Old Men?**
    A. John Hillcoat
    B. Werner Herzog
    C. Michael Bay
    D. the Coen brothers

3. **Which McCarthy work was the turning point in helping him achieve mainstream acclaim?**
    A. No Country for Old Men
    B. The Road
    C. Blood Meridian
    D. The Orchard Keeper

4. **What type of job did McCarthy take while living in Chicago and working on his first novel?**
    A. editor
    B. waiter
    C. auto mechanic
    D. taxi driver

5. **The Road was published in what year?**
    A. 1907
    B. 1973
    C. 2006
    D. 2009

6. **Which of the following are personified in the novel?**
    A. darkness and sadness
    B. happiness and sadness
    C. death and darkness
    D. death and happiness

7. **What is the meaning of "secular"?**
   A. not pertaining to religion
   B. confused
   C. agnostic
   D. pertaining to religion

8. **The man and the boy discover what abandoned invention in the woods, which symbolizes the futility of man's efforts in the face of the universe's indifference?**
   A. sextant
   B. railroad tracks
   C. train
   D. truck

9. **Elijah the prophet ascends to heaven in what?**
   A. balloon
   B. chariot of fire
   C. chariot of horses
   D. angel's wings

10. **In the novel, the man has a flashback in which all clocks stop at what time?**
    A. 1:17
    B. 2:17
    C. 17:10
    D. 11:17

11. **The man finds which of the following two items in a field, one of which he gives to the boy?**
    A. Coca Cola and coin
    B. rare rock and arrowhead
    C. coin and rare rock
    D. coin and arrowhead

12. **What is the purpose of a sextant?**
    A. determining one's location
    B. calculating time of lunar eclipses
    C. increasing fertility
    D. navigating a ship's course

13. **At the beach, the boy makes a figure of what in the sand?**
  A. map of streets
  B. mermaid
  C. indecipherable letters
  D. sand castle

14. **What is of particular ambiguity about the arrow man?**
  A. his fate
  B. his name
  C. his motives
  D. his family members

15. **The man uses which of the following figures of speech?**
  A. Kick the bucket.
  B. Wave a white flag.
  C. As the crow flies.
  D. Break a leg.

16. **Which of the following is not an aspect of McCarthy's prose?**
  A. sentence fragments
  B. obscure vocabulary
  C. proper punctuation
  D. run-on sentences

17. **The Road is told primarily in which narrative point of view?**
  A. third person
  B. first person
  C. second person
  D. none of the above

18. **Directly before the man's death, what do he and the boy talk about?**
  A. prayer
  B. the little boy
  C. the pistol
  D. the son's fate

19. **What is the denouement of the novel?**
    A. The boy is rescued by the man with a shotgun.
    B. The protagonists arrive at the coastline.
    C. The man dies.
    D. The trout survive.

20. **What do the man and the boy do when they see a group of people, followed by wagons and slaves, coming up the road?**
    A. They ignore the small army of people.
    B. They hide.
    C. They confront the small army of people.
    D. They run away.

21. **What is the first thing the boy gives to Ely?**
    A. a jacket
    B. can of fruit
    C. shoes
    D. glass of wine

22. **The man suggests to Ely that his son could be:**
    A. the youngest person on earth
    B. a good guy
    C. a prophet
    D. a god

23. **When the man and the boy find the train, how far away are they (in terms of time) from the sea?**
    A. 2-3 weeks
    B. 2-3 months
    C. 1 week
    D. 1 month

24. **What causes the father to snap at his son uncharacteristically?**
    A. The son accidentally shoots the man with a bow and arrow.
    B. The son complains about being hungry.
    C. The son does not quickly retrieve the first-aid kit.
    D. The son cries too loudly.

25. **For how many days does the boy remain by his father's body?**

A. one day
B. four days
C. three days
D. seven days

Quiz 4 Answer Key

1. **(B)** lightning
2. **(D)** the Coen brothers
3. **(C)** Blood Meridian
4. **(C)** auto mechanic
5. **(C)** 2006
6. **(C)** death and darkness
7. **(A)** not pertaining to religion
8. **(C)** train
9. **(B)** chariot of fire
10. **(A)** 1:17
11. **(D)** coin and arrowhead
12. **(A)** determining one's location
13. **(A)** map of streets
14. **(A)** his fate
15. **(C)** As the crow flies.
16. **(C)** proper punctuation
17. **(A)** third person
18. **(B)** the little boy
19. **(A)** The boy is rescued by the man with a shotgun.
20. **(B)** They hide.
21. **(B)** can of fruit
22. **(D)** a god
23. **(A)** 2-3 weeks
24. **(C)** The son does not quickly retrieve the first-aid kit.
25. **(C)** three days

20860559R00071

Printed in Great Britain
by Amazon